P9-BJC-723

GOODMAN'S FIVE-STAR STORIES

MORE ADVENTURES

10 More Tales of Adventure
With Exercises to Help You Read and Write

by Burton Goodman

Glencoe McGraw-Hill

New York, New York   Columbus, Ohio   Chicago, Illinois   Peoria, Illinois   Woodland Hills, California

JAMESTOWN EDUCATION

TITLES IN THE SERIES

Adventures	Level B	After Shocks	Level E
More Adventures	Level B	Sudden Twists	Level F
Chills	Level C	More Twists	Level F
More Chills	Level C	Encounters	Level G
Surprises	Level D	More Encounters	Level G
More Surprises	Level D	Conflicts	Level H
Shocks	Level E	More Conflicts	Level H

Glencoe/McGraw-Hill

A Division of The McGraw·Hill Companies

Acknowledgements are on page 140, which is to be considered an extension of this copyright page.

ISBN : 0-89061-825-9

Send all Inquiries to:
Glencoe/McGraw-Hill
8787 Orion Place
Columbus, OH 43240

8 9 10 11 12 116 / 055 09 08 07 06 05

Contents

To the Student

Here are ten more exciting *Adventures.* I have picked these stories because I like them very much. I think that you will like them too. They are tales that come from around the world.

These tales will be fun to read. And the exercises will be fun to do too. They will help you read and write better. And you will learn some important literature skills.

Study the vocabulary words before you read the story. They will help you understand the story. Later, do the exercises after each of the TALES:

TELL ABOUT THE STORY.

ADD WORDS TO SENTENCES.

LEARN NEW WORDS.

EXPLAIN WHAT HAPPENED.

SPOT STORY ELEMENTS.

TELL ABOUT THE STORY helps you find key facts in a story. Sometimes these facts are called *details.*

ADD WORDS TO SENTENCES builds your reading and vocabulary skills. This part uses fill-in, or cloze, exercises.

LEARN NEW WORDS builds your vocabulary skills. Often, you can work out the meaning of a new word. You can do this by looking at the words *around* the new word. When you do this, you are using *context clues.* The vocabulary words in each story are printed in **dark type.** You may look back at these words when you answer the vocabulary questions.

EXPLAIN WHAT HAPPENED builds your *critical thinking* skills. You will have to think about what happened in the story. Then you must figure out the answers.

Spot story elements helps you understand important elements of literature. Some story elements are *plot, character,* and *setting.* On page 3 you will find the meanings of these words. You may look back at the meanings when you answer the questions.

Another part, **THINK SOME MORE ABOUT THE STORY** gives you a chance to think, talk, and *write* about the story.

There are four questions for each of the **TALES** exercises. Here is the way to do the exercises:

- Do all the exercises.

- Check your answers with your teacher.

- Use the scoring chart at the end of each exercise to figure out your score for that exercise. Give yourself 5 points for each right answer. (Since there are four questions, you can get up to 20 points for each exercise.)

- Use the **TALES** scoring chart at the end of the exercises to add up your total score. If you get all the questions right, your score will be 100.

- Keep track of how well you do. First write your Total Score on the **Progress Chart** on page 138. Then write your score on the **Progress Graph** on page 139. Look at the **Progress Graph** to see how much you improve.

I know that you will like reading the stories in this book. And the exercises after the **TALES** will help you read and write better.

Now . . . get ready for some *More Adventures.*

Burton Goodman

The Short Story— Important Words

Character: a character is someone in a story. The writer tells you what the character is like. The way a character looks, speaks, and acts *characterizes* that person.

Main Character: the person the story is mostly about.

Plot: what happens in a story. The first thing that takes place in a story is the first thing in the *plot*. The last thing that takes place in the story is the last thing in the plot.

Setting: where and when the story takes place. The *setting* is the time and the place of the story.

1
The Wish Ring

by Anna Eichberg

Before You Read

Before you read "The Wish Ring," study the words below. Make sure you know what each word means. This will help you understand the story.

eagle: a large bird

greedy: when one wants something too much (money, for example)

manage: to be able to do something

grave: As used in this story, the word means "a place in the earth for a dead body."

fortune: good luck; much money or riches

The Wish Ring

by Anna Eichberg

A young farmer was cutting hay in his field. The day was warm and the work was hard. He stopped to have lunch. He sat under a tree to eat his meal of bread and cheese.

Just then he saw an old woman. She was coming down the road. She was so old that she could hardly walk. She looked hungrily at the farmer's food.

He said to her, "Rest here for a while. I will **share** my bread and cheese with you."

She sat and ate. Soon she felt better. She said to the farmer, "You have been kind to me. Now I will be kind to you." She showed him a path. Then she said, "Walk for two days along this road. You will come to a tree that is very tall. It is taller than all of the other trees. If you can cut it down, you will have good luck."

The farmer picked up his ax. He began to walk. Sure enough, after two days he saw the tree. He cut it down. As it fell, a nest with two eggs dropped to the earth.

An eagle flew out of one egg. And out of the other egg rolled a ring. The eagle **sailed** into the air. As it

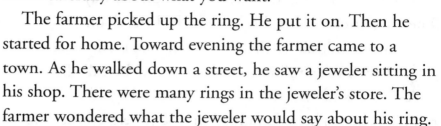

did, it cried out, "Take the ring! Put it on your finger and turn it once. It will give you a wish. But remember this! The ring can give you only one wish! So think carefully about what you want!"

The farmer picked up the ring. He put it on. Then he started for home. Toward evening the farmer came to a town. As he walked down a street, he saw a jeweler sitting in his shop. There were many rings in the jeweler's store. The farmer wondered what the jeweler would say about his ring.

So the farmer asked, "How much do you think this ring is worth?"

The jeweler looked at the ring. He said, "It is not worth anything."

The farmer laughed. "This ring is worth more than *all* of your rings. It is a wish ring. When you turn the ring, it gives one wish."

The jeweler was greedy. He thought to himself, "I would like to have that ring. It would make me rich!" He told the farmer, "You are tired. You have had a long trip. Why don't you rest here tonight?"

He gave the farmer a meal and a place to stay. That night the farmer fell fast asleep. The jeweler came into the room in the middle of the night. He took the ring off the farmer's finger. In its place he put a ring that looked like the wish ring.

The next morning the farmer went on his way. The jeweler closed his shop. He locked the door. He stood in the middle of the room. Then he turned the ring. "I wish for a million pieces of gold," he called.

As soon as he said those words, pieces of gold came raining down. The gold landed on the jeweler's head. Gold poured over his arms and back. The weight of the gold broke the floor. And the jeweler and his money fell down to the cellar.

The loud noise surprised the neighbors. They ran to the jeweler's shop. They found him dead under his pile of gold.

When the farmer got home, he was filled with joy. He showed the ring to his wife. He said, "This is a wish ring. But we can have only one wish. We must think very carefully about what we want."

She said, "Why don't we wish for the piece of land that is next to our field?"

"Let us not wish for that," the husband said. "We can work very hard for a year. Then we will have enough money to buy the land."

So the two worked very hard. At the end of the year, they had enough money to buy the land.

"See," said the man. "We have the land. And we still have the wish!"

The wife said, "We need a horse and a cow. What do you think about wishing for them?"

"A horse and a cow! Let us not waste the wish on that. We will manage to get a horse and a cow."

And in a year's time they had saved the money for the horse and the cow. The man was pleased. He said, "We got what we wanted. And we still have the wish. How lucky we are!"

"Yes, dear husband. But there is something we do not have. We do not have children. Could we wish for them?"

The farmer said, "I, too, want children. But why don't we wait a little while longer."

The next year they had a baby son. And in the years after that, they had three more children.

But now the farmer's wife talked about using the wish. She said, "You work so hard. And you could be a gentleman with bags of gold. You could be a king."

He answered, "We are young. And life is long. There is only one wish in the ring. Who knows when we may really need that wish. Is there anything we want? Have we not done well since we got the ring? Let us wait for a while."

And so that was the end of the matter. For it really seemed as if the ring had brought them good luck. The farmer and his wife were doing very well. The farmer built more barns. They were always full. And in a few years, he became a rich man. Still, he worked in the fields as if he had to earn his pay.

And the years went by.

Sometimes, when they were alone, the farmer's wife would speak to her husband about the ring. She would say, "There are some things that we might do." But he always answered, "We still have time. Anyway, the best things come last." Finally, she did not speak of the ring again.

It is true that the farmer often looked at the ring. He turned it around on his finger as many as twenty times a day. But he was very careful never to make a wish.

After many years, the farmer and his wife grew old. They never used the wish. And then, on the same night, they both **peacefully** died.

The **weeping** children and grandchildren stood by the graves. One daughter wanted to take the ring from her father's hand. She wanted it to remember him by. But the oldest son said, "Let our father take his ring into the grave. There was some story about the ring. They never said what it was. But our mother often looked at the ring. Perhaps she gave it to him when they were young."

So the old farmer was buried with the ring. It was supposed to be a wish ring, but it was not. Yet it brought as much good fortune as anyone could want.

TELL ABOUT THE STORY.

Put an *x* in the box next to the right answer. Each sentence tells a *fact* about the story.

1. The eagle said that the ring would give
   ☐ a. one wish.
   ☐ b. two wishes.
   ☐ c. three wishes.

2. The jeweler wished for
   ☐ a. a large piece of land.
   ☐ b. a horse and a cow.
   ☐ c. a million pieces of gold.

3. The farmer's wife wanted her husband to wish for
   ☐ a. a new house.
   ☐ b. fine clothing.
   ☐ c. children.

4. After the farmer became rich, he
   ☐ a. stopped working.
   ☐ b. kept working in his fields.
   ☐ c. was no longer kind.

ADD WORDS TO SENTENCES.

Complete the sentences below. Fill in each blank with one of the words in the box. Each word can be found in the story. There are five words and four blanks. This means that one word in the box will not be used.

Here is _____ that is fun to
                    1

try. You may be _____ by what
                            2

you find. Ask ten people this question:

"If you had one _____, what
                              3

would it be?" See how many people

_____, "I would wish for a
        4

hundred wishes."

wish	something
evening	
answer	surprised

☐ X 5 = ☐

NUMBER   YOUR
CORRECT   SCORE

☐ X 5 = ☐

NUMBER   YOUR
CORRECT   SCORE

LEARN NEW WORDS.

The vocabulary words are printed in **dark type** in the story. You may look back at the words before you answer these questions. Put an *x* in the box next to the right answer.

1. The farmer was willing to share his food. The word *share* means
   - ☐ a. buy.
   - ☐ b. ask for.
   - ☐ c. give some away.

2. The eagle sailed into the air. The word *sailed* means
   - ☐ a. flew.
   - ☐ b. fell.
   - ☐ c. followed.

3. That night the husband and wife both peacefully died. The word *peacefully* means
   - ☐ a. angrily.
   - ☐ b. quietly.
   - ☐ c. loudly.

4. The weeping children loved their mother and father. The word *weeping* means
   - ☐ a. crying.
   - ☐ b. fighting.
   - ☐ c. singing.

☐ × 5 = ☐

NUMBER CORRECT   YOUR SCORE

EXPLAIN WHAT HAPPENED.

Here is how to answer these questions. First think about what happened in the story. Then *figure out* (work out) the right answer. This is called *critical thinking*.

1. The old woman helped the farmer because
   - ☐ a. she liked the way he looked.
   - ☐ b. he gave her money.
   - ☐ c. he gave her some food.

2. Which sentence is true?
   - ☐ a. The farmer asked for gold.
   - ☐ b. The children sold the ring.
   - ☐ c. The jeweler was killed by his wish.

3. The farmer sometimes turned the ring 20 times a day. He probably
   - ☐ a. was trying to take off the ring.
   - ☐ b. often thought about making a wish.
   - ☐ c. did not like the ring.

4. The story makes the point that you can get what you want by
   - ☐ a. working hard.
   - ☐ b. wishing for it.
   - ☐ c. being lucky.

☐ × 5 = ☐

NUMBER CORRECT   YOUR SCORE

SPOT STORY ELEMENTS.
Some story elements are **plot,
character,** and **setting.** (See
page 3.) Put an *x* in the box
next to the right answer.

1. What happened first in the *plot*?
   - ☐ a. The jeweler gave the farmer food.
   - ☐ b. A farmer met an old woman.
   - ☐ c. The farmer grew rich.

2. What happened last in the *plot*?
   - ☐ a. The jeweler gave the farmer a place to stay.
   - ☐ b. The farmer and his wife died.
   - ☐ c. A ring rolled out of the egg.

3. Which sentence best describes (tells about) the *character* of the farmer?
   - ☐ a. He worked very hard.
   - ☐ b. He was lazy.
   - ☐ c. He did not love his wife.

4. The story is *set*
   - ☐ a. in the middle of a city.
   - ☐ b. on a road.
   - ☐ c. on and around a farm.

☐ X 5 = ☐

NUMBER   YOUR
CORRECT   SCORE

THINK SOME MORE
ABOUT THE STORY.
Your teacher might want you to
write your answers.
- Why do you think the farmer never made a wish?
- Suppose the farmer had made a wish as soon as he got home. What would have happened? How do you think the story would have ended?
- What lesson or lessons does the story teach?

Write your scores in the boxes below.
Then write your scores on pages 138
and 139.

☐ **T**ELL ABOUT THE STORY
+
☐ **A**DD WORDS TO SENTENCES
+
☐ **L**EARN NEW WORDS
+
☐ **E**XPLAIN WHAT HAPPENED
+
☐ **S**POT STORY ELEMENTS
=
☐ TOTAL SCORE: Story 1

15

2
The Lady in Black

by O. Henry

Before You Read

Before you read "The Lady in Black," study the words below. Make sure you know what each word means. This will help you understand the story.

count: in Europe, a count is a man from a rich and important family

accident: something unlucky that happens without warning

locket: a small case used for holding a picture

remind: to make someone think of, or remember, something

wedding: the event at which two people get married

invite: to ask someone to join you at a place

The Lady in Black

by O. Henry

Have you heard of O. Henry? He wrote more than three hundred short stories. They all end with a surprise. This one takes place in 1907. Try to guess the surprise.

Andy Walters lived in an apartment in New York City. One day a young woman moved into his building. Her name was Miss Conway. She had just come to New York.

Miss Conway seemed quiet and **shy.** Andy always said hello when he saw her in the hall. But Miss Conway kept to herself. He hardly knew that she was around.

One Sunday Andy was leaving his room. Just then he saw Miss Conway coming down the hall. She was wearing a dress that was as black as night. Her hat was black. Her gloves were black too. Andy had never thought of Miss Conway as pretty. But against the black dress, her gray eyes seemed to **glow.** She seemed almost beautiful.

"It is a lovely afternoon, Miss Conway," he said.

"Yes," she said. Her voice was sad. "It is lovely to those who can enjoy it, Mr. Walters."

Andy said, "I see that you are dressed all in black. I hope that . . . that no one in your family has died."

Miss Conway did not answer at once. Then she said slowly, "Someone has died. He was not in my family. He was someone who . . . who. . . . But why should I trouble you with my problems, Mr. Walters?"

"Trouble me?" said Andy. "It is no trouble at all."

Miss Conway smiled a little smile. Andy thought that even her smile was sad.

She said, "There is an old saying, Mr. Walters. 'Laugh and the world laughs with you. Cry and you cry alone.' I have learned that well, Mr. Walters. I have learned that very well. I have no friends in this city. But you have been kind. You always say hello when we meet."

Andy said, "It is hard to be alone in New York. That is so. But when this town gets to know you, it becomes very friendly. Why don't we take a little walk in the park? That might make you feel better."

"Thank you, Mr. Walters. A little walk would be nice. But I hope you don't mind listening to someone whose sad heart is breaking."

They went outside together and walked to the park. They sat down on a quiet bench near a tree.

"We were going to be married," said Miss Conway. "We were going to be married next spring. It may sound funny, but he was a real count. He owned a lot of land and a castle in Italy. Count Fernando Mazzini was his name."

Miss Conway put a handkerchief up to her eyes. "At first Papa said that I could not marry the count. But then Fernando showed him some papers. They **proved** that he owned the land and a castle and had a lot of money. Finally, Papa said we could get married next spring."

Miss Conway's voice began to break. "Papa and Fernando went to Italy. They wanted to fix up the castle for me. Before Fernando left, he tried to give me a few thousand dollars. But Papa said no. That's the way Papa is. He would not let me take a ring or any presents from Fernando. And when they left for Italy, I came to the city. I thought I would work in New York for a while before I joined them."

Miss Conway **paused** for a moment. Then she went on. "Yesterday I got a letter from Italy. Fernando is dead. He has been killed in an accident on his boat.

"That is why I am wearing black, Mr. Walters. My heart is breaking. I am no fun to be with. I cannot take an interest in anyone. Now would you like to walk back?"

"I am very sorry," Andy said softly. "No, let's not walk back just yet. And do not say you have no friends in this city, Miss Conway. I am very sorry. And I want you to believe that I am your friend."

"I have his picture here," said Miss Conway. "I keep it in this locket. I never show it to anyone. But I will show it to you because I believe you are a true friend."

Andy looked for a long time at the picture that Miss Conway showed him. The count's face was interesting to look at. It was strong and smart. It was the face of a man who looked like he could lead others.

"I have a bigger picture in my room," said Miss Conway. "I will show it to you. They are all that I have to remind me of Fernando. But he will always be in my heart."

They walked back to the building. There Miss Conway showed Andy the large picture of the count. Again, Andy studied the picture she showed him.

She said, "He gave me this on the night that he left for Italy. I had the one in my locket made from this one."

"He is a fine looking man," Andy said. He did not speak for a minute. Then he said, "Would you care to take another walk with me next Sunday?"

Two months later Andy and Miss Conway made plans to get married. Still, Miss Conway kept wearing black.

A little while after that, the two were sitting on the same bench in the park. It was evening. The trees looked beautiful in the moonlight. But Andy was very quiet. He hardly said a word.

"What is the matter, Andy? You seem so different tonight."

"It is nothing, Maggie."

"I know better. I know you too well. Tell me. What is it?"

"It is nothing much, Maggie."

"Yes, it is. I want to know. Are you thinking about somebody else? Please tell me, Andy."

"I will tell you then," said Andy. "But I guess you won't understand it. You have heard of Mike Dolan, haven't you, Maggie? Everyone calls him 'Big Mike' Dolan."

"No, I have not," said Maggie. "And I do not want to—not if he is why you are acting this way."

"He is one of the most important men in New York. He knows the mayor and the governor, too. Say one bad word about Big Mike, and you'll be sorry for the rest of your life.

"Well, Big Mike is a friend of mine. I mean we are not really close friends. But we are friends good enough. He is as good a friend to a poor man as he is to a rich man. I met him today on the street. And what do you think he did? He came up to me and shook my hand. He said, 'Andy, I hear that you are getting married. Be sure to ask me to come to the wedding. I want to come. So be sure to invite me!'

"You may not understand it, Maggie. But I would like to have Big Mike come to our wedding. I *want* him to come! I would cut off one of

my hands to have him there! That is why I am looking a little troubled tonight."

"Why don't you just invite him then?" said Maggie.

"I cannot," Andy said sadly. "There is a reason why I cannot. Do not ask me what it is. I cannot tell you. But he must not be there!"

"Oh, I do not care," said Maggie. "You have your reasons, I guess. But why can't you smile at me tonight?"

"Maggie," Andy said after a while. "Do you think as much of me as you did of your—as you did of Count Mazzini?"

Andy waited a long time. But Maggie did not answer. And then, suddenly, she threw her arms around his neck. She began to cry and to shake.

"There, there, now," Andy said softly. "Tell me what it is."

"Andy," said Maggie. "I have lied to you. And you will never marry me or love me anymore. But I feel that I have to tell you. Andy, there never was a count. I have never had a boyfriend in my life. But all the other girls had. They always talked about them. And that seemed to make the fellows like them even more.

"And Andy, I look good in black—you know that I do. So I went to a store and bought that picture. And I had a little one made up for my locket. I made up the story about the count. I said he died so that I could wear black. Oh, Andy, nobody can love someone who tells lies. You will leave me now, Andy, and I will be sorry. Oh, there was never anybody I liked but you!"

But Andy did not push Maggie away. He put his arms around her and held her closer. She looked up and saw that he was smiling.

"Could you—could you forgive me, Andy?"

"Sure," said Andy. "Everything is all right now. You have taken care of that! I was hoping you would before the wedding. And you have. You have! It's wonderful, Maggie!"

"Andy," said Maggie, when she finally felt better. "Did you believe the story about the count?"

"Not really," said Andy. "You see, it is Big Mike Dolan's picture you have in your locket."

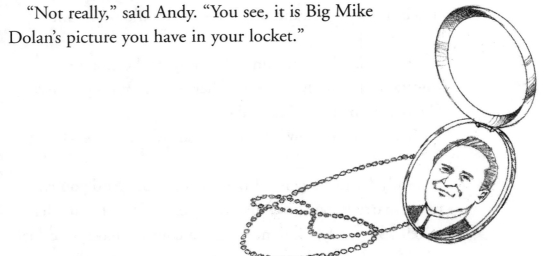

TELL ABOUT THE STORY.

Put an *x* in the box next to the right answer. Each sentence tells a *fact* about the story.

1. Miss Conway said that she
   - ☐ a. loved the city.
   - ☐ b. had many friends in the city.
   - ☐ c. had no friends in the city.

2. Andy asked Miss Conway to
   - ☐ a. have dinner with him.
   - ☐ b. take a walk in the park.
   - ☐ c. go for a ride.

3. Miss Conway told Andy that the count
   - ☐ a. did not love her anymore.
   - ☐ b. lost all of his money.
   - ☐ c. had been killed.

4. Mike Dolan said he wanted to
   - ☐ a. come to Andy's wedding.
   - ☐ b. help Andy get a new job.
   - ☐ c. help Andy meet important people.

ADD WORDS TO SENTENCES.

Complete the sentences below. Fill in each blank with one of the words in the box. Each word can be found in the story. There are five words and four blanks. This means that one word in the box will not be used.

"The Lady in Black" is like many

of O. Henry's other _____.
_1_

It has just a _____ characters,
_2_

and it is very short. It takes place

in New York, the _____
_3_

O. Henry loved. And like all of

O. Henry's stories, it _____
_4_

with a surprise.

picture	few
	stories
ends	city

☐ × 5 = ☐

NUMBER CORRECT   YOUR SCORE

☐ × 5 = ☐

NUMBER CORRECT   YOUR SCORE

27

LEARN NEW WORDS.

The vocabulary words are printed in **dark type** in the story. You may look back at the words before you answer these questions. Put an *x* in the box next to the right answer.

1. Miss Conway seemed quiet and shy. The word *shy* means
   - ☐ a. very brave.
   - ☐ b very rich.
   - ☐ c easily frightened.

2. Against the black dress, her eyes seemed to glow. The word *glow* means
   - ☐ a. cry.
   - ☐ b. close.
   - ☐ c. look bright.

3. The papers proved that he owned land. The word *proved* means
   - ☐ a. asked questions about.
   - ☐ b. showed that something was true.
   - ☐ c. was hard to read.

4. She paused before she began to speak. The word *paused* means
   - ☐ a. stopped.
   - ☐ b. laughed.
   - ☐ c. sat down.

EXPLAIN WHAT HAPPENED.

Here is how to answer these questions. First think about what happened in the story. Then *figure out* (work out) the right answer. This is called *critical thinking.*

1. Which sentence is true?
   - ☐ a. The count loved Maggie very much.
   - ☐ b. The count owned a castle.
   - ☐ c. Maggie made up the story about the count.

2. Why did Maggie say the count had died?
   - ☐ a. She wanted to wear black.
   - ☐ b. She stopped loving him.
   - ☐ c. She got the news in a letter.

3. We may infer (figure out) that Andy knew Maggie was lying when he
   - ☐ a. saw her in the hall.
   - ☐ b. spoke to her father.
   - ☐ c. looked at the picture she showed him.

4. At the end of the story, Andy felt
   - ☐ a. very sad.
   - ☐ b. very happy.
   - ☐ c. angry with Maggie.

☐ X 5 = ☐

NUMBER CORRECT   YOUR SCORE

☐ X 5 = ☐

NUMBER CORRECT   YOUR SCORE

SPOT STORY ELEMENTS.

Some story elements are **plot**, **character**, and **setting**. (See page 3.) Put an *x* in the box next to the right answer.

1. What happened first in the *plot*?
   - ☐ a. Andy told Maggie about Mike Dolan.
   - ☐ b. Maggie moved into Andy's building.
   - ☐ c. Maggie showed Andy a picture.

2. What happened last in the *plot*?
   - ☐ a. Andy met Mike Dolan in the street.
   - ☐ b. Maggie told Andy that she had lied about the count.
   - ☐ c. Maggie said that the count was rich.

3. Where is the story *set*?
   - ☐ a. Chicago
   - ☐ b. New Jersey
   - ☐ c. New York City

4. The story is *set*
   - ☐ a. in 1907.
   - ☐ b. about ten years ago.
   - ☐ c. today.

☐ × 5 = ☐

NUMBER CORRECT   YOUR SCORE

THINK SOME MORE ABOUT THE STORY.

Your teacher might want you to write your answers.

- Why did Miss Conway tell Andy the story about the count? Give as many reasons as you can.
- Andy looked "for a long time" at the picture Miss Conway showed him. Why did Andy look at the picture for such a long time?
- At first, Andy could not ask Mike Dolan to come to the wedding. Explain why.

Write your scores in the boxes below. Then write your scores on pages 138 and 139.

☐ **T**ELL ABOUT THE STORY
+
☐ **A**DD WORDS TO SENTENCES
+
☐ **L**EARN NEW WORDS
+
☐ **E**XPLAIN WHAT HAPPENED
+
☐ **S**POT STORY ELEMENTS
=
☐ TOTAL SCORE: Story 2

3
Good Advice

by Joe Hayes

Before You Read

Before you read "Good Advice," study the words below. Make sure you know what each word means. This will help you understand the story.

coin: a piece of money made of metal. A penny is a coin.

to be on guard: to watch out for or be very careful of

disappeared: was suddenly gone

monster: a large, frightening animal

hissing: a sound like *sssss*. Some snakes make a hissing sound.

foolish: silly

Good Advice

by Joe Hayes

This is the story of a man and his wife. They had one son. Everyone liked the boy. He was very nice. But sometimes he was a little slow when it came to learning things.

One day the parents spoke to the boy. The father said, "You know that we are very poor. You must go out and look for work. You must bring home some money for the family."

So the boy went out to look for work. Soon he came to a farm. He got a job working there. At the end of the month, they paid him one silver dollar.

The boy started for home. He was planning to give the money to his parents.

On the way home the boy met an old man. The man had a long gray beard.

The boy greeted the man. *"Buenas tardes,"*[1] said the boy. "What are you doing here on the road?"

The man told the boy, "I am selling advice."

"Advice?" said the boy.

"Yes," said the man. "Advice—wise words that can help you."

The man said to the boy, "If you give me one silver coin, I will give you good advice."

The boy handed the coin to the man. The old man whispered in his ear:

"Dondequiera que fueras,
haz lo que vieras."

("Wherever you may go,
do as you see others do.")

The boy walked home. He kept **repeating** that advice over and over to himself. "Wherever you may go, do as you see others do."

When he got home, the boy told his parents what had happened.

"What?" said his father. "You spent your silver coin on a piece of advice?"

His parents were angry. They **scolded** the boy. They told him to go back to work.

[1] **Buenas tardes:** the Spanish words for "good afternoon"

The boy went back to the farm. He worked for another month. They gave him another silver dollar. Again he started for home.

Again he met the old man. The old man said, "I have some more good advice for you. This second bit of advice is even better than the first."

The boy gave the man the silver coin. The old man told him these words:

"Si eres casado,

que tenga cuidado."

("If you are a married man,

be on your guard.")

The boy walked home. He kept on saying that advice over and over to himself. He said, "If you are a married man, be on your guard."

When the boy got home, his parents were very angry. "Silly boy!" they said. "We **depended** on you to help us with the money you made. And you have given it away for advice. Here is some more advice! Go back to work! And do not come home until you have some money to give us!"

They sent the boy out of the house. He went back to the farm. You can guess what happened. He worked for another month. Then he took his silver coin and started for home. Again he met the old man on the road. But this time the boy did not give the money away at once.

The boy was worried. He said, "If I **spend** this money, I cannot go home."

"Money! What is money?" said the old man. "Money comes and money goes. But good advice will last you all your life. There is nothing more important than good advice."

So the boy gave his coin to the old man. And the old man gave him this advice:

"Aunque pobre, eres sano;
trabaja con la mano."

("Although poor, you are a healthy man. Earn your living with your hands.")

As soon as the old man finished speaking, he disappeared. The boy thought, "Now I cannot go home again. I will go out into the world. I will do the best I can."

The boy traveled for a long time. He came to a city. In the middle of the city was a castle. He made his way to the castle gate. There he saw soldiers. They were marching back and forth. They had rifles on their shoulders.

Suddenly, the boy remembered the advice he had bought. The old man had said, "Wherever you may go, do as you see others do." The boy said to himself, "I must do what I see being done."

The boy had no rifle. So he picked up a broom. It was standing against a wall. He put the broom on his shoulder. Then he joined the soldiers.

At that moment the princess was looking out her window. There is something you should know about the princess. She was very, very sad. She had not laughed for many years. Her father, the king, said that any man who made the princess laugh could marry her.

The princess saw the boy pick up the broom. She saw him put it on his shoulder. She saw him march along with the soldiers. When she saw all this, she began to laugh. She laughed and laughed. The king heard her laugh. He sent for the boy. He was brought to the castle at once.

There is something else you should know. There was a reason that the princess was so sad. She had been married a hundred times. But each of her husbands had disappeared on their wedding night. They were never seen again! People said they were eaten by some terrible monster!

The boy was married to the princess. After the wedding, they went to the princess's room. Then the boy remembered the second bit of advice. The old man had said, "If you are a married man, be on your guard."

The boy thought to himself, "Now I am a married man. I'd better be careful. I will stay awake all night. I will be on my guard."

At midnight he was beginning to fall asleep. Suddenly, he heard a hissing sound. He opened his eyes. Two feet from his face was a giant snake! Its mouth was open. Its eyes were yellow. It had a long red tongue.

The boy jumped up. He grabbed a sword that was hanging on the wall. He hit the snake until it died. That snake had eaten the other men. But now it was dead!

In the morning everyone saw that the princess's husband was still alive. They were very happy. The king said, "We must have a very big party!"

The party lasted for seven days and seven nights. But the boy kept thinking about the old man's last bit of advice. The old man had said, "Although poor, you are a healthy man. Earn your living with your hands."

The boy told his wife, "This party is very nice. It is fun to dance and to eat. But I think I should be working with my hands. Tomorrow I will look for work."

"But you are married to a princess," said his wife. "You do not have to work."

He said, "Your money is yours. I must earn my own."

There was another king. He lived not far away. The boy went to the palace of that king. The boy asked for work, and they gave him a job. He had to build a wall with some other workers.

The workers saw that the boy did not know how to build a wall. They thought that he seemed a little foolish. The workers made fun of him.

Finally, the boy got angry. He told the workers, "You can say what you like. But I am married to a princess. Can any of you say that?"

Of course the workers did not believe a word he said. One of them went to the king. The worker said, "The boy makes up stories. He says he is married to a princess."

The king got angry. He sent for the boy. But when he saw the boy, the king started to laugh. "So!" said the king. "You say you are a prince."

"No, your Majesty," answered the boy. "But my wife is a princess."

The king laughed even louder.

The boy told him, "If you do not believe me, wait until noon. You will see her when she brings me my lunch."

The king got angry again. "Yes," he said. "I will wait until noon. But if I do not see a princess bring you lunch, you will spend the rest of your life in jail."

"Fine," said the boy. "And if you do see a princess, what will you give me?"

The king smiled. He said, "If *you* are married to a princess, I will give you your weight in gold!"

The boy went back to work on the wall. At twelve o'clock he called to the workers, "Look! Here comes my wife!"

A carriage came up the road. It was pulled by twelve white horses. In front of the horses rode fifty soldiers. Behind the carriage rode fifty more soldiers. The carriage stopped in front of the workers. Then the princess came out of the carriage.

The king was watching from his window. When he saw the princess, he got very angry again. But there was nothing he could do. He had to pay the boy the gold.

The boy was weighed. Then the king gave the boy his weight in gold. The boy went back to the castle with the princess. And they lived there happily for the rest of their lives.

But he always said to anyone who would listen, "I owe everything I have to good advice."

TELL ABOUT THE STORY.

Put an *x* in the box next to the right answer. Each sentence tells a *fact* about the story.

1. The boy gave his pay to
   - ☐ a. his mother and father.
   - ☐ b. an old man.
   - ☐ c. the princess.

2. The princess's husbands were killed by
   - ☐ a. the king.
   - ☐ b. some soldiers.
   - ☐ c. a snake.

3. The boy got a job
   - ☐ a. building a wall.
   - ☐ b. cutting down trees.
   - ☐ c. giving good advice.

4. The king had to give the boy
   - ☐ a. a silver dollar.
   - ☐ b. a few coins.
   - ☐ c. his weight in gold.

ADD WORDS TO SENTENCES.

Complete the sentences below. Fill in each blank with one of the words in the box. Each word can be found in the story. There are five words and four blanks. This means that one word in the box will not be used.

Joe Hayes _____ his living
  by telling stories. He has been doing
  that for _____ than twenty
  years. He has _____ tales like
  "Good Advice" in hundreds of
  schools. If you _____ "Good
  Advice," you will probably like the
  stories in his book *The Day It Snowed Tortillas.*

told	earns
happened	
liked	more

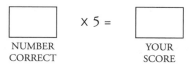

NUMBER CORRECT   × 5 =   YOUR SCORE

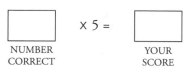

NUMBER CORRECT   × 5 =   YOUR SCORE

41

LEARN NEW WORDS.

The vocabulary words are printed in **dark type** in the story. You may look back at the words before you answer these questions. Put an *x* in the box next to the right answer.

1. He kept repeating the old man's advice. The word *repeating* means
   - ☐ a. forgetting.
   - ☐ b. selling.
   - ☐ c. saying over.

2. They scolded him because he did not bring home any money. The word *scolded* means
   - ☐ a. thanked.
   - ☐ b. tried to help.
   - ☐ c. talked angrily to.

3. They depended on the boy to help. The word *depended* means
   - ☐ a. counted on.
   - ☐ b. did not like.
   - ☐ c. listened to.

4. He said, "If I spend the money, I cannot go home." The word *spend* means
   - ☐ a. save or keep.
   - ☐ b. pay or use up.
   - ☐ c. look for and find.

EXPLAIN WHAT HAPPENED.

Here is how to answer these questions. First think about what happened in the story. Then *figure out* (work out) the right answer. This is called *critical thinking*.

1. The old man believed that
   - ☐ a. money was as important as good advice.
   - ☐ b. only money was important.
   - ☐ c. good advice was more important than money.

2. The princess laughed at the boy because he
   - ☐ a. told funny stories.
   - ☐ b. looked funny with a broom.
   - ☐ c. was wearing funny clothes.

3. When the workers saw the princess, they were probably
   - ☐ a. surprised.
   - ☐ b. sad.
   - ☐ c. worried.

4. Which sentence is true?
   - ☐ a. The boy did not like to work.
   - ☐ b. The boy's parents were kind.
   - ☐ c. The old man's advice helped the boy very much.

[ ] X 5 = [ ]

NUMBER CORRECT   YOUR SCORE

[ ] X 5 = [ ]

NUMBER CORRECT   YOUR SCORE

Spot Story Elements.

Some story elements are **plot**, **character**, and **setting**. (See page 3.) Put an *x* in the box next to the right answer.

1. What happened first in the *plot*?
   - ☐ a. The boy killed the snake.
   - ☐ b. The boy married the princess.
   - ☐ c. The boy went to work on a farm.

2. What happened last in the *plot*?
   - ☐ a. The boy met an old man.
   - ☐ b. The king saw the princess come out of the carriage.
   - ☐ c. The workers made fun of the boy.

3. Who is the *main character*?
   - ☐ a. the boy
   - ☐ b. the old man
   - ☐ c. the princess

4. Which sentence best describes (tells about) the *character* of the boy?
   - ☐ a. He was afraid to travel.
   - ☐ b. He was very lazy.
   - ☐ c. He listened to and used the old man's advice.

☐ X 5 = ☐

NUMBER CORRECT   YOUR SCORE

Think Some More About the Story.

Your teacher might want you to write your answers.

- Do you think the boy's parents were right to get angry with their son? Why? Should they have told him not to come home until he had money? Explain.
- Why did the workers think that the boy was making up stories?
- The writer said the boy was sometimes "a little slow when it came to learning things." What did the boy say to the king that showed that the boy could be smart?

Write your scores in the boxes below. Then write your scores on pages 138 and 139.

☐ **T**ELL ABOUT THE STORY
+
☐ **A**DD WORDS TO SENTENCES
+
☐ **L**EARN NEW WORDS
+
☐ **E**XPLAIN WHAT HAPPENED
+
☐ **S**POT STORY ELEMENTS
=
☐ TOTAL SCORE: Story 3

4
A River Story

by Ellen C. Babbitt

Before You Read

Before you read "A River Story," study the words below. Make sure you know what each word means. This will help you understand the story.

island: land that has water all around it

ripe: when a piece of fruit has finished growing and is ready to eat

choking: not able to take in air

crawl: to move slowly by pulling the body along the ground

trap: A trap is used to catch an animal or a person.

fear: to feel afraid of

A River Story

by Ellen C. Babbitt

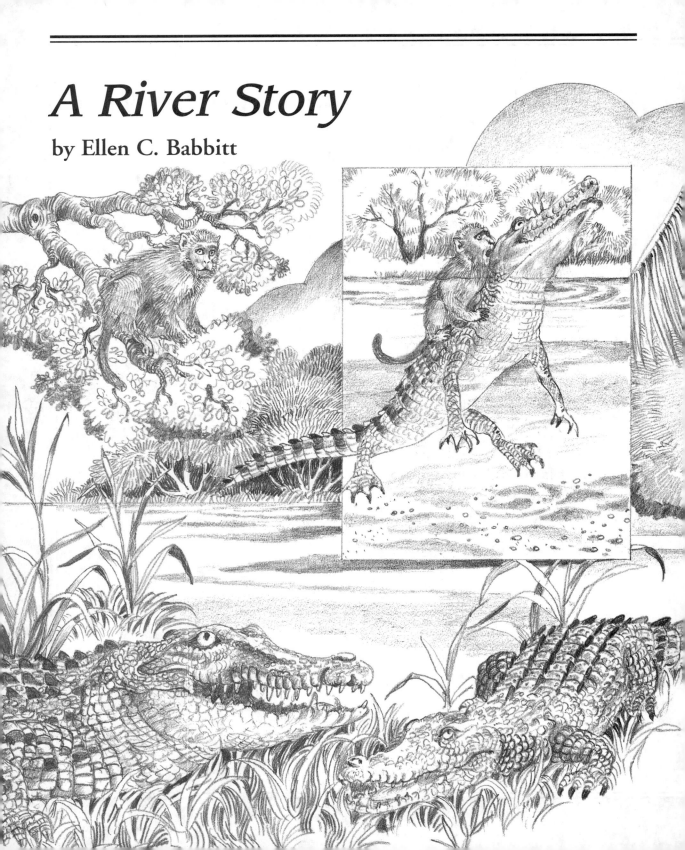

A monkey lived in a tall tree next to a river.

There were many crocodiles in the river. A crocodile watched the monkey day after day. Finally, the crocodile said to her son, "My boy, you must get that monkey for me. I want to eat the heart of a monkey. A monkey's heart is very good food."

The little crocodile asked, "But how can I catch a monkey? I do not travel on land. And the monkey does not go into the water."

"Think about it," said the mother. "Think very hard. You will find a way."

The little crocodile thought and thought. He thought for a long time.

At last he said to himself, "I know how I can get that monkey. There is an island in the middle of the river. There is ripe fruit on the island, and the monkey likes ripe fruit. I know what I will do."

So the crocodile swam to the tree where the monkey lived. But the crocodile was not too smart.

"Oh, monkey," he called. "Come with me. Let us go to that island where the ripe fruit grows."

"How can I go with you?" the monkey asked. "I cannot swim."

"No, but I can. I will take you there on my back," the crocodile said.

The monkey loved ripe fruit. He wanted it very much. So he hopped down from the tree. Then he jumped onto the crocodile's back.

"Off we go!" the little crocodile said.

"This is a fine ride you are giving me!" the monkey said.

"Do you think so?" the crocodile asked. "Well, how do you like *this*?" The crocodile **dived** under the water.

"Oh, don't!" cried the monkey, as he went down. He was afraid that he would drown. He could not let go. But he could not **breathe** while he was under the water.

When the crocodile came up, the monkey was choking.

"Why did you take me under the water?" the monkey asked.

"I am going to drown you," the crocodile said. "My mother wants to eat the heart of a monkey. I am going to take your heart to her."

The monkey said, "You should have told me you wanted my heart! Then I would have brought it with me."

"That is strange," the little crocodile said. "Do you mean that you left your heart back there in the tree?"

"That is just what I mean," the monkey said. "If you want my heart, we must go back to the tree. That is where it is."

The monkey thought for a moment. Then he said, "But we are near the island where the ripe fruit grows. Why don't you take me there first?"

"Oh, no, monkey," said the crocodile. "I will take you straight back to your tree. Climb up the tree. Get your heart and bring it to me. Then we will see about going to the island."

"Well, all right," the monkey said.

The crocodile swam back near the tree. The monkey jumped off the crocodile's back. As soon as the monkey was on land, he climbed to the top of the tree.

He looked down at the crocodile below. "My heart is way up here," the monkey yelled. "If you want it, come up here and get it!"

The little crocodile often swam by that tree. He kept an eye on the

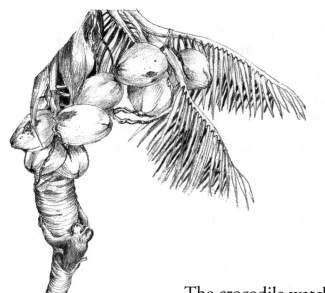

monkey. The monkey wanted some **peace.** He moved to another tree. It was far down the river.

But the little crocodile found the monkey. He saw him in his new tree. It was near the island with the fruit.

There was a very big rock in the water. It was between the island and the tree. The monkey could jump onto the rock. Then he jumped onto the island. He stayed there all day, eating the fruit.

The crocodile watched this from far away. He thought to himself, "The monkey stays on the island all day. But I will catch him when he goes home at night."

The monkey was eating fruit on the island. He was having a fine time. The crocodile swam about. He watched the monkey all day.

Toward night the crocodile crawled out of the water. He climbed onto the big rock. The crocodile did not move. He lay there very still.

When it got dark, the monkey got ready to go home. He stared at the rock. Then he stopped.

"Something is the matter with that rock," the monkey said to himself. "I never saw it so high." Then he thought, "I know! The crocodile is lying on the rock!"

The monkey went to the edge of the water. He called, "Hello! Hello, rock!"

There was no answer.

Then he called again, "Hello, rock!"

Three times the monkey called. Then he said, "Why is it, friend rock, that you do not answer me tonight?"

"Oh," said the silly crocodile to himself. "The monkey speaks to the rock. And the rock answers the monkey. This time I will have to answer for the rock."

So the crocodile answered, "Yes, monkey. What is it?"

The monkey laughed. Then he said, "Oh, it is you, crocodile. It *is* you, isn't it?"

"Yes," said the crocodile. "I am waiting here for you. I am going to eat you."

"This time you have caught me in a trap," the monkey said. "There is no other way for me to get home. Open your mouth wide so that I can jump into it."

The monkey knew that when crocodiles open their mouths wide, they always shut their eyes.

The crocodile lay on the rock with his mouth wide open. His eyes were shut tight. Then the monkey jumped.

But not into the crocodile's mouth. Oh, no! He jumped onto the top of the crocodile's back. From there he jumped onto the land. Then he hopped up into his tree.

The crocodile **realized** that the monkey had played a trick on him. The crocodile called out, "Monkey, you are very smart. And you have no fear. I will leave you alone from now on."

The monkey said, "Thank you, crocodile. But I think I will watch out for you just the same anyway!"

TELL ABOUT THE STORY.

Put an *x* in the box next to the right answer. Each sentence tells a *fact* about the story.

1. The crocodile asked her son to bring her
   - ☐ a. some fruit.
   - ☐ b. a rock.
   - ☐ c. a monkey's heart.

2. The little crocodile planned to
   - ☐ a. help the monkey.
   - ☐ b. drown the monkey.
   - ☐ c. give the monkey some food.

3. The monkey said that his heart was
   - ☐ a. on an island.
   - ☐ b. in his body.
   - ☐ c. in the tree.

4. At the end of the story, the monkey jumped on top of the crocodile's
   - ☐ a. back.
   - ☐ b. head.
   - ☐ c. tail.

ADD WORDS TO SENTENCES.

Complete the sentences below. Fill in each blank with one of the words in the box. Each word can be found in the story. There are five words and four blanks. This means that one word in the box will not be used.

Crocodiles have _____, low bodies with very short legs. They use their strong tails to help them

_____. A crocodile's eyes are at the _____ of its head. That makes is easy for the _____ to see as it moves through the water.

crocodile	afraid
top	
swim	long

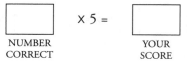

NUMBER CORRECT   × 5 =   YOUR SCORE

NUMBER CORRECT   × 5 =   YOUR SCORE

53

LEARN NEW WORDS.

The vocabulary words are printed in **dark type** in the story. You may look back at the words before you answer these questions. Put an *x* in the box next to the right answer.

1. The crocodile dived under the water. The word *dived* means
   - ☐ a. went up.
   - ☐ b. went down.
   - ☐ c. went away from.

2. He could not breathe under the water. The word *breathe* means
   - ☐ a. talk.
   - ☐ b. smile.
   - ☐ c. take in air.

3. The monkey wanted some peace, so he moved to another tree. The word *peace* means
   - ☐ a. quiet.
   - ☐ b. friends.
   - ☐ c. food.

4. The crocodile realized that the monkey had played a trick on him. The word *realized* means
   - ☐ a. knew or understood.
   - ☐ b. wished for or wanted.
   - ☐ c. shouted or called.

EXPLAIN WHAT HAPPENED.

Here is how to answer these questions. First think about what happened in the story. Then *figure out* (work out) the right answer. This is called *critical thinking.*

1. Which sentence is true?
   - ☐ a. Crocodiles cannot swim.
   - ☐ b. When crocodiles open their mouths, they keep their eyes open.
   - ☐ c. The monkey loved ripe fruit.

2. The monkey made believe that he
   - ☐ a. spoke to the rock.
   - ☐ b. could not climb trees.
   - ☐ c. was able to swim.

3. We may infer (figure out) that the crocodile
   - ☐ a. never caught the monkey.
   - ☐ b. finally caught the monkey.
   - ☐ c. became the monkey's friend.

4. The last sentence of the story shows that the monkey
   - ☐ a. believed the crocodile.
   - ☐ b. did not believe the crocodile.
   - ☐ c. was going to move to another tree the next day.

☐ X 5 = ☐
NUMBER   YOUR
CORRECT   SCORE

☐ X 5 = ☐
NUMBER   YOUR
CORRECT   SCORE

SPOT STORY ELEMENTS.

Some story elements are **plot**, **character**, and **setting**. (See page 3.) Put an *x* in the box next to the right answer.

1. What happened first in the *plot*?
   - ☐ a. The crocodile took the monkey under the water.
   - ☐ b. The crocodile climbed onto the big rock.
   - ☐ c. The monkey moved away.

2. Which sentence best describes (tells about) the *character* of the crocodile?
   - ☐ a. He was silly, but he sometimes had good ideas.
   - ☐ b. He was very, very smart.
   - ☐ c. He liked to travel on land.

3. Which sentence best *characterizes* the monkey?
   - ☐ a. He liked to go into the water.
   - ☐ b. He never left his tree.
   - ☐ c. He tricked the crocodile two times.

4. The story is *set*
   - ☐ a. in a zoo.
   - ☐ b. by a river.
   - ☐ c. on a farm.

NUMBER CORRECT   × 5 =   YOUR SCORE

THINK SOME MORE ABOUT THE STORY.

Your teacher might want you to write your answers.
- Explain how the crocodile tricked the monkey.
- Tell all the ways the monkey tricked the crocodile.
- Who do you think was smarter—the crocodile or the monkey? Explain your answer.

Write your scores in the boxes below. Then write your scores on pages 138 and 139.

☐ **T**ELL ABOUT THE STORY
+
☐ **A**DD WORDS TO SENTENCES
+
☐ **L**EARN NEW WORDS
+
☐ **E**XPLAIN WHAT HAPPENED
+
☐ **S**POT STORY ELEMENTS
=
☐ TOTAL SCORE: Story 4

5
The Wild Winds of Wok

by Dorothy Tofte

Before You Read

Before you read "The Wild Winds of Wok," study the words below. Make sure you know what each word means. This will help you understand the story.

arrive: to come to a place

planet: Planets move around the sun. Some planets are bigger than Earth.

dome: a building with a large, round roof

allow: to let someone do something

breeze: a light, soft wind

shake: to move back and forth very fast

The Wild Winds of Wok

by Dorothy Tofte

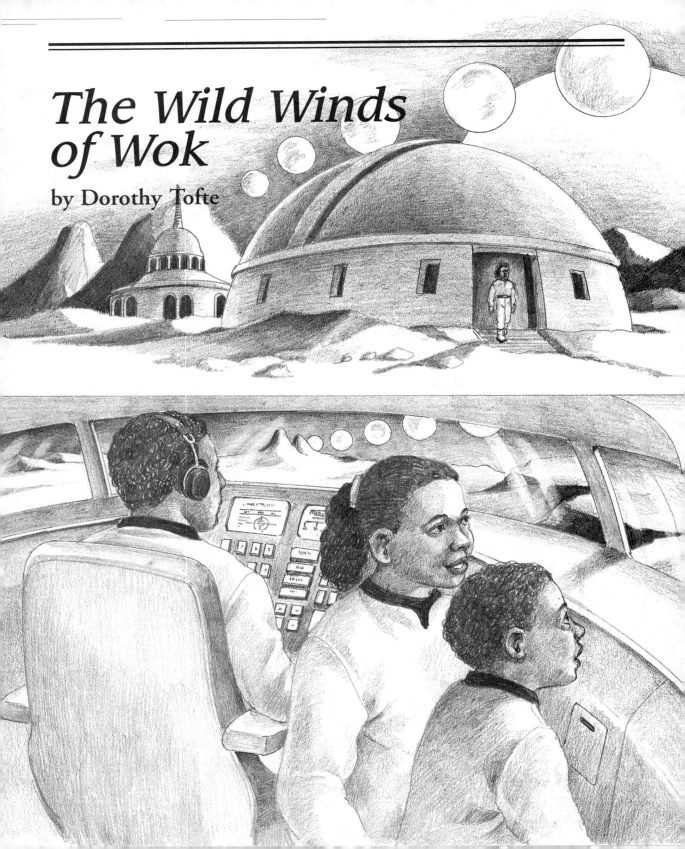

The spaceship was coming down. It was landing on the strange world of Wok. Vala and her younger brother, Jac, looked out the window.

"It looks very peaceful to me," Vala said. She pointed to the open fields. There were people working.

"Yes," answered Jac. "But remember what Father said. We cannot be outside when the wild winds come. I do not understand why they come at all."

Vala smiled. "You can ask Father about that when we arrive. He explained it to me once. He said that Wok is a good planet to live on. The people like it there. The only bad thing is that it has five moons."

"Why is that bad?" asked Jac.

Before Vala could answer, a voice rang out. It said, "Please **prepare** to land. In thirty seconds we will be on the ground."

A few minutes later Vala and Jac were on their way to the place where visitors stayed. It was a big building. It had a large, round roof. Father called the building "the dome."

"Why are five moons bad?" Jac asked again, as they moved toward the dome.

Vala pointed up at the sky over Wok. She said, "On Earth we have only one moon. Wok has five moons. Two times each month they all line up in a row. The pull from the moons causes what people call 'the wild winds of Wok.' I do not know how long the winds last. But the people of Wok have to stay inside on that day. And visitors have to stay inside the dome."

They reached the door of the dome. Vala looked up at the sky again. She said, "I think that the 'wild winds' are supposed to come tomorrow."

Jac sighed. "That was a long ride in the spaceship from Earth. I was hoping to go out tomorrow. I wanted to look around. I wanted to see what this planet is like."

Vala shook her head. "They will not allow anyone to go out tomorrow," she said.

What Vala did not count on was her own love of adventure. The next morning she was up very early. Everyone else was asleep. Most of the people on Wok slept late on the days when the wild winds came. And the visitors inside the dome also slept late.

Vala was very **curious.** She looked outside. Everything seemed calm. Vala looked around. No one was there. She slipped quietly out the door of the dome. She went just a few feet away at first. It felt good to take in the fresh air. The soft ground under her feet felt good too.

There was no wind. Perhaps she was wrong. Perhaps this was not the day for the wild winds of Wok.

She took a few more steps away from the dome. It was so quiet. There was no sound at all. There was not even a breeze. What if a wind did come up? It would take her only a minute to run back to the dome.

Suddenly, Vala thought that she saw something move. What was it? She saw a small animal. It was no bigger than a kitten. Vala looked closer. She saw that it *was* a kitten!

A kitten on Wok! If only that were true. If only it were really a live kitten! Vala had looked forward to leaving Earth to join her father on Wok. The hardest part was giving up her pet cat. Vala had the cat since she was a little girl. It was the only pet that Vala ever had.

If she could catch this kitten, she could have a new pet! Vala looked up at the sky. Nothing was happening. Surely the wild winds would not come today.

Vala walked slowly toward the hole into which the kitten had gone. Vala looked down. She saw two shining yellow eyes. The hole was very deep. But it was not very wide. Vala was too large to fit into the small hole. How could she reach the kitten?

Vala looked around. A shovel with a broken handle lay on the ground. Vala picked it up and began to dig. The earth on Wok was very soft. She dug until the hole was large enough for her to fit inside. Just then she heard a loud sound. It was coming from somewhere behind her. Vala turned around.

While she had been digging, the air had filled with dust. There was so much dust that it was hard for Vala to see. The wild winds had come! They had started already!

Vala looked at the dome. It was near. Yet it was so far! The dome was large. But it was hard to see it because of all the flying dust. Vala threw the broken shovel away. She wondered what to do.

Then the door of the dome opened. Someone was standing by the door. Vala opened her eyes wide. It was her brother, Jac. He was waving to her. He was waving to her to come back!

Vala started to run toward the dome. Then she felt herself being pulled back by the wind. She fell to the ground. She tried to hold on to anything that would keep her from being carried away.

Then she remembered the hole in the ground! She tried to crawl toward it. It was only a few feet away! But the wind was very strong! She was not sure she could make it. She finally did reach it. Then she crawled inside.

She could hear the wind screaming outside. The terrible roar hurt her ears. Vala closed her eyes and stayed down.

Then she felt something soft against her. It was the kitten! Vala held it in her arms.

Vala pressed her legs against the sides of the hole. She pushed her feet down into the earth. It was the only way to keep from being pulled into the air by the wind.

She stayed that way for almost two hours. She heard the wind whistling and pounding outside. Then, suddenly, it was quiet. All sound had stopped!

Vala felt much better. She started to crawl out of the hole. But the kitten began to meow in **terror.** Vala felt its little body shaking with fear.

"It's over!" Vala said to the kitten. "It's over. It is safe to go out now."

But the kitten kept meowing in fear. Vala could tell that it was very frightened about going outside.

"It is all right now," she said softly to the kitten. The kitten still meowed with fear.

Vala thought to herself, "Maybe it knows something that I don't know. Maybe I had better wait here a little longer."

Vala made up her mind to wait. A few minutes later she heard a loud sound. The sound turned into a roar. The wild winds of Wok had come back!

Vala waited for another two hours. Then, as before, the wind suddenly stopped. One minute the roar was almost more than she could stand. The next minute there was no sound at all.

This time the kitten purred happily as Vala climbed out of the hole. Vala stood up. She looked around. The sky was clear. The air was quiet. She could smell the dust that had fallen all around. But the terrible winds had gone!

Vala looked over at the dome. The door was opening. Her father and Jac were the first to come out. They ran to Vala.

"What a silly thing to do," her father said. He pulled her into his arms and held her close. "Are you all right?"

"Yes, Father. And look. I found a kitten. So something good came out of what I did."

"A kitten?" said her father. He smiled. Then he took the small animal out of her arms. "What you call a kitten is really a baby traxta. They grow up to be like tigers back on Earth. No one on Wok has ever kept a traxta as a pet."

"Could I try?" Vala asked. "After all, it saved my life. It kept me from going out. I was ready to leave the hole when the winds stopped the first time. But then they started again."

"Yes," said her father. "That is what the winds do. They stop for a little while. Then they start again. It is a good thing you did not go out."

Jac took the baby traxta out of his father's hands. He looked at it. Then he said, "Vala was able to **escape** from the wild winds of Wok. Maybe she will be able to raise a tiger as a pet."

Their father smiled. He said to Vala, "You can keep it until the wild winds come again. Then we will see how things are working out."

Vala grinned at Jac. Her smile showed that she was sure everything would turn out all right!

TELL ABOUT THE STORY.

Put an *x* in the box next to the right answer. Each sentence tells a *fact* about the story.

1. The bad thing about Wok was that it
   - ☐ a. had five moons.
   - ☐ b. was very hot.
   - ☐ c. did not have much food.

2. Vala saw a small animal that she thought was a
   - ☐ a. tiger.
   - ☐ b. traxta.
   - ☐ c. kitten.

3. Vala saved herself from the wild winds by
   - ☐ a. running into the dome.
   - ☐ b. hurrying back to the spaceship.
   - ☐ c. getting into the hole she had dug.

4. Vala said that the small animal
   - ☐ a. saved her life.
   - ☐ b. was lost.
   - ☐ c. was hungry.

ADD WORDS TO SENTENCES.

Complete the sentences below. Fill in each blank with one of the words in the box. Each word can be found in the story. There are five words and four blanks. This means that one word in the box will not be used.

You know that the planet

_____ has only one moon. But

1

other _____ have more than

2

one moon. Jupiter, the largest planet,

has the most _____: twelve.

3

One moon is very _____. It is

4

only fourteen miles wide.

planets	small
Earth	
tomorrow	moons

☐ X 5 = ☐

NUMBER
CORRECT   YOUR
               SCORE

☐ X 5 = ☐

NUMBER
CORRECT   YOUR
               SCORE

67

LEARN NEW WORDS.

The vocabulary words are printed in **dark type** in the story. You may look back at the words before you answer these questions. Put an *x* in the box next to the right answer.

1. A voice said, "Please prepare to land." The word *prepare* means
   - ☐ a. get ready.
   - ☐ b. sit down.
   - ☐ c. stop talking.

2. Vala was curious about Wok. When you are *curious,* you
   - ☐ a. feel tired.
   - ☐ b. do not care about something.
   - ☐ c. really want to know something.

3. The small animal began to meow in terror. When you feel *terror,* you
   - ☐ a. are very pleased.
   - ☐ b. become frightened.
   - ☐ c. are interested.

4. Vala was able to escape from the wild winds. The word *escape* means
   - ☐ a. hear about.
   - ☐ b. keep warm.
   - ☐ c. get away from.

EXPLAIN WHAT HAPPENED.

Here is how to answer these questions. First think about what happened in the story. Then *figure out* (work out) the right answer. This is called *critical thinking.*

1. Which sentence is true?
   - ☐ a. The winds came every day.
   - ☐ b. The winds stopped for a while and then started again.
   - ☐ c. When the winds stopped, they did not start again.

2. By going out when the wild winds came, Vala
   - ☐ a. nearly died.
   - ☐ b. had a good time.
   - ☐ c. did a wise thing.

3. Vala could tell that the small animal
   - ☐ a. was not friendly.
   - ☐ b. did not want her to go out.
   - ☐ c. would grow up to be wild.

4. The last sentence of the story shows that Vala will probably
   - ☐ a. get caught in the wild winds again.
   - ☐ b. have to give up the traxta.
   - ☐ c. be able to keep the traxta.

☐ X 5 = ☐

NUMBER CORRECT   YOUR SCORE

☐ X 5 = ☐

NUMBER CORRECT   YOUR SCORE

68

SPOT STORY ELEMENTS.

Some story elements are **plot**, **character**, and **setting**. (See page 3.) Put an *x* in the box next to the right answer.

1. What happened first in the *plot*?
    - ☐ a. Vala climbed out of the hole in the ground.
    - ☐ b. The spaceship landed.
    - ☐ c. Jac waved to Vala to come back.

2. Who is the *main character* in the story?
    - ☐ a. Vala
    - ☐ b. Father
    - ☐ c. Jac

3. The story is *set*
    - ☐ a. on Earth.
    - ☐ b. on the moon.
    - ☐ c. on a planet called Wok.

4. The story is *set*
    - ☐ a. today.
    - ☐ b. many years ago.
    - ☐ c. years from now.

THINK SOME MORE ABOUT THE STORY.

Your teacher might want you to write your answers.
- Explain what caused the wild winds of Wok.
- Why do you think everyone on Wok slept late on the days when the wild winds came?
- Vala looked at the small animal and said, "Maybe it knows something that I don't know." Was Vala right about that? Explain.

Write your scores in the boxes below. Then write your scores on pages 138 and 139.

☐ + **T**ELL ABOUT THE STORY

☐ + **A**DD WORDS TO SENTENCES

☐ + **L**EARN NEW WORDS

☐ + **E**XPLAIN WHAT HAPPENED

☐ = **S**POT STORY ELEMENTS

☐ TOTAL SCORE: Story 5

☐ X 5 = ☐

NUMBER CORRECT   YOUR SCORE

6
Stone Soup

an old tale

Before You Read

Before you read "Stone Soup," study the words below.
Make sure you know what each word means. This will
help you understand the story.

pack: As used in this story, the word means "a kind of bag
made to be carried on the back."

valley: the low land between hills or mountains

jacket: a short coat

tossed: threw

stove: something used to cook food on

bunch: a group, or number, of things that are together

Stone Soup

an old tale

Lars woke up early one morning. He looked out the window. The sun was shining brightly.

Lars said, "It is a beautiful day, and I want to see the world. But the world is very big. I must leave at once."

Lars washed and dressed and put on good walking shoes. He ate a big breakfast. Then he found a few things he might need for his trip. He put them into a pack and put the pack on his back. Then he said, "Now I am ready to see the world."

Lars began to walk. He walked across fields. He walked over large hills and through deep valleys. He walked for a long time, but he did not see anyone.

Lars began to get tired. He said, "I must rest for a while." He sat on the ground and opened his pack. He took out some bread. He was so hungry that he ate all of the bread. Then he drank all of the water he brought.

Lars got up. He **continued** to walk. Night came. It was dark, and it began to get cold. He put on the jacket he had in his pack. Soon he saw a big tree. Its branches hung down to the ground. He found a **comfortable** place under the tree. Lars closed his eyes and soon fell asleep.

Lars slept all night. He woke up the next morning. He felt fine, but he was a little hungry. He thought, "I must keep on walking, for I want to see the world.

It is an interesting place. But I need some food. I hope that I meet someone soon."

The sun came up. It began to get warm, and Lars took off his jacket. By now it was noon. Lars came to a road. He thought to himself, "This is good. Every road goes somewhere. So I will be somewhere soon."

There were stones on the road. Lars picked up some stones. He tossed them ahead while he walked. He put one of the stones into his pocket.

Then Lars saw something far away. It looked like a house. Lars was glad. He had walked for a long time, and he was very, very hungry.

Lars went up to the house and knocked on the front door. A man came to the door.

"Can I help you?" he asked.

"Yes. My name is Lars. I am seeing the world. I have walked for a long time. Do you have some food I can eat?"

The man said, "I am poor. I have no food to **spare.** Try the next house."

Lars walked down the road to the next house. He knocked on the door. A woman answered his knock. She looked at the man.

He said, "My name is Lars. I am seeing the world. Do you have some food I can eat?"

"I am sorry," she said. "My family is poor. My husband and I have three children to feed. We do not have enough food."

"You do not have enough food? And you have three children to feed? That is sad." Lars put his hands into his pockets. Then he said, "But I think I can help."

"Help?" said the woman. "How can you help?"

"I have a soup stone," said Lars.

"A soup stone?" she asked.

"It makes wonderful soup."

"Well, then. Come in."

Lars said, "First we need a big pot. It must hold lots of soup."

"I have a large iron pot." She brought out the large pot.

"We can use that," said Lars. "We must fill it with water."

"We have plenty of water," she said.

They filled up the pot. They put the pot on the stove.

"Now for the soup stone!" said Lars.

"Wait!" said the woman. "I want my children to see. They must look at this wonder!"

So she called her three children. Just then her husband came home. They stood there and waited. Everyone looked at Lars.

He reached into his pocket and took out the stone. He held it high in the air and waved it around. Then he dropped it into the pot.

They all sat down and waited for the water to get hot. Lars got up. He looked into the pot. He said, "Everything is going very well. If we only had a few potatoes to put into the pot."

The woman said, "I think that we have some potatoes." She found some potatoes and put them into the pot.

Lars rubbed his hands together and said, "Yes, all is going well. If we only had some carrots. Carrots would be good."

The woman turned to her son and said, "Run over to our neighbor. He has a little garden. Ask him for some carrots. But be sure that you tell him about the soup stone."

The boy ran out. He came back with the neighbor. The neighbor was carrying a large bunch of carrots.

The neighbor looked at Lars. "You didn't tell me you had a soup stone!" he said. He threw the carrots into the pot.

Lars said, "Ah! Doesn't this smell good! If we only had some onions. Onions would be good."

The neighbor said, "I have a friend who has onions. I will go to his house."

The neighbor rushed out. He came back with his friend. The friend was carrying a big bag of onions. He put them into the pot.

"It is going well," said Lars. He began to **stir** the soup. "But we could use some more vegetables."

The friend said, "My sister has some vegetables. I will go and get her."

The friend came back with his sister. She was holding a basket that had some corn and some beans. They went into the pot.

"Things could not be better," said Lars. "The soup stone is working!"

Soon the stone soup was ready. There was a lot of soup. There was more than enough for everyone there. The woman and her husband ate the soup. The children ate the soup. The neighbor ate the soup. The neighbor's friend ate the soup. The friend's sister ate the soup. Lars ate the soup. And there was still some soup left.

Everyone said, "This is very good soup. I never had such good soup!"

"It is the soup stone," said Lars. "All you need is the soup stone and water. They make wonderful soup."

Lars stayed that night. But he had to leave the next day. "I must go now," he said, "for I want to see the world."

He gave the soup stone to the woman.

"You may keep this," he said. "It is my present to you."

On the road near the village, Lars found another stone. He put it into his pocket. He thought to himself, "The world is a very big place. There is so much to see. It might take me many years. But as long as I have this, I will never be hungry."

Lars whistled happily, as he went on his way.

TELL ABOUT THE STORY.

Put an *x* in the box next to the right answer. Each sentence tells a *fact* about the story.

1. Lars wanted to
   - ☐ a. see the world.
   - ☐ b. stay close to home.
   - ☐ c. make many good friends.

2. At first, the woman said she could not give Lars food because she
   - ☐ a. did not know him.
   - ☐ b. was very tired.
   - ☐ c. was poor.

3. The first thing they put in the pot was
   - ☐ a. water.
   - ☐ b. carrots.
   - ☐ c. beans.

4. When the stone soup was ready, there was
   - ☐ a. just enough for everyone.
   - ☐ b. not enough for everyone.
   - ☐ c. more than enough for everyone.

ADD WORDS TO SENTENCES.

Complete the sentences below. Fill in each blank with one of the words in the box. Each word can be found in the story. There are five words and four blanks. This means that one word in the box will not be used.

Every year people go to England to see Stonehenge's _____ stones.
₁
Some of the stones are thirty feet high and weigh more _____ fifty
₂
thousand pounds. Many _____
₃
ago the stones were placed where they now stand. But no one really knows who put the _____ there—
₄
or why.

years	neighbor
interesting	
than	stones

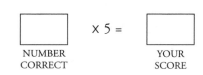

NUMBER CORRECT   × 5 =   YOUR SCORE

NUMBER CORRECT   × 5 =   YOUR SCORE

79

LEARN NEW WORDS.

The vocabulary words are printed in **dark type** in the story. You may look back at the words before you answer these questions. Put an *x* in the box next to the right answer.

1. Lars was tired, but he continued to walk. The word *continued* means
   - ☐ a. fell down.
   - ☐ b. stopped suddenly.
   - ☐ c. kept on going.

2. He fell asleep in a comfortable place under the tree. Something that is *comfortable*
   - ☐ a. feels good.
   - ☐ b. is hard to find.
   - ☐ c. costs a lot of money.

3. The man said he had no food to spare. The word *spare* means
   - ☐ a. to buy.
   - ☐ b. to be able to give.
   - ☐ c. to cook.

4. Lars began to stir the soup. The word *stir* means
   - ☐ a. to move around or mix.
   - ☐ b. to kick or hit.
   - ☐ c. to talk about or speak.

EXPLAIN WHAT HAPPENED.

Here is how to answer these questions. First think about what happened in the story. Then *figure out* (work out) the right answer. This is called *critical thinking*.

1. We may infer (figure out) that the soup was very good because
   - ☐ a. there was a soup stone in it.
   - ☐ b. it had a lot of water.
   - ☐ c. it was filled with good things to eat.

2. Which sentence is true?
   - ☐ a. Many people helped make the stone soup.
   - ☐ b. Nobody liked the stone soup.
   - ☐ c. The people believed that Lars had tricked them.

3. Everyone thought the stone soup
   - ☐ a. was wonderful.
   - ☐ b. was too hot.
   - ☐ c. was too sweet.

4. At the end of the story, Lars felt
   - ☐ a. surprised.
   - ☐ b. happy.
   - ☐ c. hungry.

	X 5 =	
NUMBER CORRECT		YOUR SCORE

	X 5 =	
NUMBER CORRECT		YOUR SCORE

80

SPOT STORY ELEMENTS.
Some story elements are **plot**,
character, and **setting**. (See
page 3.) Put an *x* in the box
next to the right answer.

1. What happened last in the *plot*?
   - ☐ a. Lars fell asleep under a
     tree.
   - ☐ b. Lars gave the soup stone
     to the woman.
   - ☐ c. A friend put some onions
     in the soup.

2. Who is the *main character* in the
   story?
   - ☐ a. Lars
   - ☐ b. the woman who owned
     the pot
   - ☐ c. the neighbor

3. Which sentence best *characterizes*
   Lars?
   - ☐ a. He was not very smart.
   - ☐ b. He did not like to walk.
   - ☐ c. He thought of a clever
     way to get food.

4. The story is *set*
   - ☐ a. in a store.
   - ☐ b. in a house in the country.
   - ☐ c. in a busy city.

	X 5 =	
NUMBER CORRECT		YOUR SCORE

**THINK SOME MORE
ABOUT THE STORY.**
Your teacher might want you to
write your answers.
- Why were all the people willing
  to put something into the pot?
  Think of as many reasons as you
  can.
- Why was Lars sure that he would
  never be hungry again?
- What lesson or lessons does the
  story teach?

Write your scores in the boxes below.
Then write your scores on pages 138
and 139.

☐	**T**ELL ABOUT THE STORY
+	
☐	**A**DD WORDS TO SENTENCES
+	
☐	**L**EARN NEW WORDS
+	
☐	**E**XPLAIN WHAT HAPPENED
+	
☐	**S**POT STORY ELEMENTS
=	
☐	TOTAL SCORE: Story 6

7
The Tale of the Wolf

by Lin Yutang

Before You Read

Before you read "The Tale of the Wolf," study the words below. Make sure you know what each word means. This will help you understand the story.

grateful: wanting to give thanks for something good that happens

scared: frightened or afraid

of course: yes; surely

stump: the bottom part of a tree that is left after the rest of the tree has been cut off

ox: a large animal, like a cow, that is often used for farm work

replied: answered

The Tale of the Wolf

by Lin Yutang

Many years ago, General Ho was hunting in a woods in China. The general was carrying a bow and some arrows. He walked by some trees and came to a road. In the middle of the road, he saw a wolf.

The general shot an arrow and **wounded** the wolf. It began to run. The general chased the animal, but it ran into the forest.

At that moment, a Mr. Yee was traveling through the woods. He was on his way to a nearby town. He rode on a donkey and carried a bag. In the bag were some books.

Mr. Yee was a very kind man. He loved all living things, animals, and people.

Yee heard a loud noise. Then he saw the wolf running toward him. Yee felt sorry for the wolf. He saw an arrow sticking out of the animal's back.

"Do not worry," said Yee. "I will take out the arrow for you."

"You are very kind," said the wolf. "You are a good man. A hunter is coming after me. Let me hide in your bag until he has gone. I will be grateful to you forever if you save my life."

"Poor wolf," said Yee. "I will be glad to help you. I will do what I can."

Yee **removed** the arrow. He took the books out of his bag and put them behind a tree. Then he tried to put the wolf into his bag. But the wolf was large, and the bag was small. Yee pushed and pushed. When the wolf's head went in first, his back legs and his tail stuck out. When the wolf's tail went in first, his front paws and his head stuck out.

Yee tried again and again. But he could not get the wolf into the bag.

"Hurry! The hunter is near!" cried the wolf. "Tie me up. Then push me into the bag. I think I will fit into the bag that way."

The wolf lay down on the ground. Yee tied the wolf's body and legs together. Yee pushed and pushed. He finally got the wolf into the bag. Then he lifted the bag onto his donkey's back.

Yee saw a few drops of blood on the ground. He quickly covered the blood with some earth and leaves. Just as he finished, a man came by. It was General Ho.

The general said, "Have you seen a wolf?"

"No," said Yee. "I have not seen a wolf. Wolves are very smart. He must be hiding somewhere."

The general looked closely at Yee. The general said, "He was coming this way. Anyone who tries to help the animal get away will be very sorry."

Yee said, "If I see him anywhere, I will let you know. Good luck!"

General Ho went on his way. A few minutes later, the wolf called out, "Hurry! Let me out of this bag! There is not enough air! It is hard to breathe!"

Yee quickly helped the wolf out of the bag. Then he untied the wolf.

The wolf said, "I am not badly hurt. You have saved my life. Will you do something else for me now?"

"I will be glad to help," said Yee. "What do you want me to do?"

"I am very hungry," said the wolf. "I really am **starved**."

"Yes?"

"I have not eaten for three days. And if I die tonight, you will have saved me for nothing. Why don't you let me eat you up? I am not asking too much, am I?"

Now Yee was scared. The wolf opened its mouth. It had large, sharp teeth. The wolf jumped at Yee.

Yee ran around to the other side of the donkey. Yee was shaking. He was very frightened. "You cannot do this to me!" he cried.

"Why not?"

"You cannot! I have just saved your life!"

The wolf began to chase Yee. They kept running around and around the donkey.

"Listen," Yee finally said, "let us talk about this. You think it is all right for you to eat me now. But I think it is wrong to do that. Don't you want to know that if you eat me up, you are doing the right thing?"

"Of course," said the wolf. "But I am very hungry. I am tired of all this talk. What do you think we should do?"

"Let us stop three people," said Yee. "Let us ask them what they think. But we must tell them that I saved your life!"

"All right," said the wolf. "Everyone knows that people were made to be eaten by wolves. We are much stronger than you. You are too weak to save yourself. Everyone knows that!"

They walked down the road, but there was no one there. It was late, and it was getting dark.

"I am very hungry," said the wolf. "I cannot wait much longer."

The wolf pointed to the stump of a tree by the side of the road.

"Let us ask him," said the wolf.

"But he is only a piece of tree," said Yee. "What does he know?"

"No one else is around," said the wolf. "Ask him. He will give you an answer."

Yee told the stump how he had saved the wolf's life. Yee said, "And remember this. If General Ho had found out what I did, he might have killed me. So is it right that the wolf should eat me now? Is that fair?"

A voice came out of the stump. It said, "Let me tell you my story. I am a tree. I mean I was once a tall apple tree. For twenty years I had fruit. A gardener and his family lived off my fruit. He gave some of my fruit to his friends and sold some of my fruit in the market. For twenty years he made money from the fruit that I grew. Now I am old and no longer have fruit. The gardener cut off my branches and cut most of me down. He sold me for firewood. All I am now is a stump. Ah, well, that is life. That is the way things are. Why shouldn't the wolf eat you up?"

"You see!" said the wolf. "His words are wise."

The wolf opened his mouth. He got ready to eat Yee.

"Wait! Wait a minute!" said Yee. "We must hear what two others say."

"All right," said the wolf. "But I am hungry. Let's hurry."

They walked on for a little while. Then they saw an old ox resting against a fence. The ox looked very tired.

"Ask this fellow," said the wolf. "See what he says."

Yee told his story to the ox. Then Yee said, "What do you think?"

The ox thought for a while. Then he said, "Look at me. I am old and thin. But you should have seen me when I was young. A farmer bought me at the market to work on his farm. I did most of the work. I pulled heavy things and **plowed** the land. I worked harder than the three men who worked on the farm. Because of me, the farmer did very well. He made a lot of money.

"But now I am old. The farmer makes me sleep out in the open. At night it is windy, and I get very cold. I do not mind. Everybody must get old. But the other day the farmer was talking to his wife. I heard the farmer say, 'That ox cannot work anymore. Let us not give him any more food.'"

The ox looked at Yee. "Ah, well," said the ox. "That is life! The farmer does not care about everything I did for him. So why should the wolf not eat you up?"

The wolf smiled. It opened its mouth and got ready to eat Yee.

"Not yet!" said Yee. "We must still hear one more."

They soon saw an old man. He was walking slowly down the road. He needed a stick to help him move along.

Yee was happy to see a man. Yee ran to him. "You can save my life, old man!" said Yee. "Please listen to me!"

Yee told the old man the story. The old man turned to the wolf. "He saved your life!" said the man. "And you wish to eat him now! You cannot do such a thing. That is wrong!"

"But you have not heard *my* story," answered the wolf. "Please listen to me. This man tied me up. Then he pushed me into a bag. It was terrible there. I could not breathe. There was no air! I thought I would die!"

"Well, then," said the old man. "The man is also wrong."

The old man turned to Yee. "You say you saved the wolf's life. But the wolf says you hurt him very much. I do not know who is right."

The old man turned to the wolf. "I must see for myself how you felt in the bag."

"You will see! You will see!" said the wolf. So he let himself be tied up again. Then he let himself be pushed into the bag.

"It is terrible in here!" said the wolf. "You see what I mean!"

"I see," said the old man. "That is true."

"Let me out now," called the wolf, "so I can eat up the man!"

"But I do not wish to be eaten by a wolf!" replied Yee.

"That is also true," said the old man. "I do not know what to do. I must think about this. I must think about this for a while."

So the old man and Yee both walked down the road. They left the wolf in the bag. And that took care of the question of who was right.

TELL ABOUT THE STORY.

Put an *x* in the box next to the right answer. Each sentence tells a *fact* about the story.

1. To get the wolf into the bag, Mr. Yee had to
    - ☐ a. shout at the wolf.
    - ☐ b. tie up the wolf.
    - ☐ c. make the wolf close its eyes.

2. The wolf had not eaten for
    - ☐ a. three days.
    - ☐ b. five days.
    - ☐ c. a week.

3. The ox said that the farmer
    - ☐ a. cared about him very much.
    - ☐ b. was going to let him sleep in the barn.
    - ☐ c. was not going to give him any more food.

4. At the end of the story, the wolf
    - ☐ a. ran away.
    - ☐ b. let himself be pushed into the bag.
    - ☐ c. ate Mr. Yee.

ADD WORDS TO SENTENCES.

Complete the sentences below. Fill in each blank with one of the words in the box. Each word can be found in the story. There are five words and four blanks. This means that one word in the box will not be used.

Have you ever heard the

_____ of a wild wolf at night?
₁

It is a sound that is very _____.
₂

Wolves like to _____ together.
₃

So when a _____ calls, it is
₄

usually trying to find other wolves.

> minute   call
> frightening
> travel   wolf

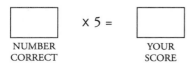

NUMBER CORRECT   x 5 =   YOUR SCORE

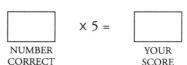

NUMBER CORRECT   x 5 =   YOUR SCORE

LEARN NEW WORDS.

The vocabulary words are printed in **dark type** in the story. You may look back at the words before you answer these questions. Put an *x* in the box next to the right answer.

1. The arrow wounded the wolf. The word *wounded* means
   - ☐ a. hurt.
   - ☐ b. hunted.
   - ☐ c. helped.

2. He removed the arrow from the wolf. The word *removed* means
   - ☐ a. looked at.
   - ☐ b. lost.
   - ☐ c. took out.

3. The wolf was starved because it had not eaten for a long time. The word *starved* means
   - ☐ a. very strong.
   - ☐ b. very hungry.
   - ☐ c. very wise.

4. The ox pulled heavy things and plowed the land. The word *plowed* means
   - ☐ a. grew.
   - ☐ b. ate.
   - ☐ c. dug up.

EXPLAIN WHAT HAPPENED.

Here is how to answer these questions. First think about what happened in the story. Then *figure out* (work out) the right answer. This is called *critical thinking*.

1. It is fair to say that the old man
   - ☐ a. saved Mr. Yee's life.
   - ☐ b. thought the wolf was right.
   - ☐ c. did not like Mr. Yee.

2. The wolf thought that people
   - ☐ a. were stronger than wolves.
   - ☐ b. were very friendly.
   - ☐ c. were weaker than wolves.

3. We may infer (figure out) that the stump and the ox thought
   - ☐ a. it was all right for the wolf to eat the man.
   - ☐ b. the wolf should not eat the man.
   - ☐ c. they had lived easy lives.

4. Which sentence is probably true?
   - ☐ a. The wolf got out of the bag.
   - ☐ b. The wolf did not get out of the bag.
   - ☐ c. General Ho killed the wolf.

☐ × 5 = ☐	
NUMBER CORRECT YOUR SCORE	

☐ × 5 = ☐	
NUMBER CORRECT YOUR SCORE	

SPOT STORY ELEMENTS.

Some story elements are **plot, character,** and **setting.** (See page 3.) Put an *x* in the box next to the right answer.

1. What happened first in the *plot*?
   - ☐ a. The old man and Mr. Yee walked down the road.
   - ☐ b. General Ho chased the wolf.
   - ☐ c. The ox told the story of his life.

2. Which sentence best *characterizes* Mr. Yee?
   - ☐ a. He was very kind.
   - ☐ b. He did not care about animals or people.
   - ☐ c. He was not afraid of anything.

3. Where is the story *set*?
   - ☐ a. in the United States
   - ☐ b. in a large town
   - ☐ c. in a woods in China

4. The story is *set*
   - ☐ a. two or three years ago.
   - ☐ b. many years ago.
   - ☐ c. today.

☐ × 5 = ☐

NUMBER CORRECT   YOUR SCORE

THINK SOME MORE ABOUT THE STORY.

Your teacher might want you to write your answers.

- Explain why the stump and the ox did not care if the wolf ate Mr. Yee.
- Do you think the stump and the ox were right? Tell why.
- Did you think the story had a good ending? Explain your answer.

Write your scores in the boxes below. Then write your scores on pages 138 and 139.

☐ **T**ELL ABOUT THE STORY
+
☐ **A**DD WORDS TO SENTENCES
+
☐ **L**EARN NEW WORDS
+
☐ **E**XPLAIN WHAT HAPPENED
+
☐ **S**POT STORY ELEMENTS
=
☐ TOTAL SCORE: Story 7

8

The Tailor's Daughter

by Parker Fillmore

Before You Read

Before you read "The Tailor's Daughter," study the words below. Make sure you know what each word means. This will help you understand the story.

agree: to feel the same way as another person does about something; to get along well with another person

truth: something that is true

dawn: the very beginning of the day, when the sun comes up

give birth: to have a baby

pole: a long, thin piece of wood

The Tailor's Daughter

by Parker Fillmore

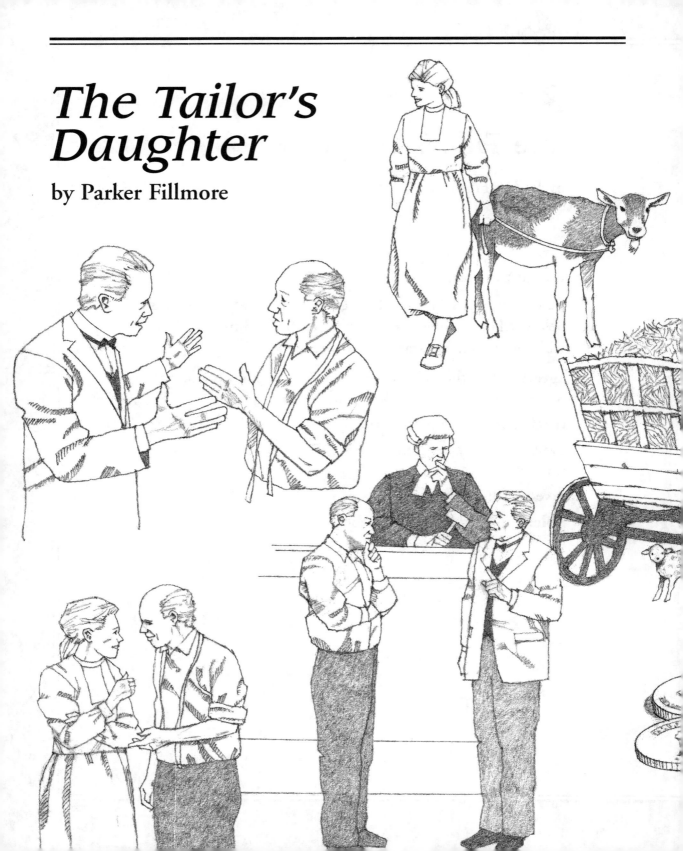

A young judge lived in a town in Finland. He was wise and kind. Everyone liked him very much. Sometimes people could not agree about something. Then they went to see the judge. He was always able to **settle** the question.

One day two old friends got into a fight. One was a rich banker. The other was a poor tailor. Each man said that he was smarter than the other.

The banker told the tailor, "If you were smart, you would be rich."

The tailor said, "Being rich does not make a man smart." Then the tailor asked, "Can you make a suit?"

The banker said, "When I need a suit made, I will go to a tailor."

"See!" said the tailor. "You must come to me!"

They went on and on that way. Finally, the banker said, "Why don't we speak to the judge? Let us see what *he* says."

The tailor said, "At last you have said something smart!"

So they went off to see the young judge. The banker said, "If the judge says you are smarter than I am, I will give you five pieces of silver."

The tailor said, "And if the judge picks you, I will make a fine dress for your wife."

The judge listened to the two men. Then he said, "I will ask you three questions. Give me your answers tomorrow at this time. They will help me **decide.**"

What could the men do? They both said, "All right."

The judge said, "Here are my questions. What is the fastest thing in the world? What is the sweetest? What is the richest?"

The banker went home. He thought about the questions. He could not think of good answers. He told his wife the three questions.

She said, "Why nothing in the world is faster than our own gray horse. Nothing ever passes us on the road. And nothing is sweeter than the honey I buy in the store."

"Yes," said her husband. "But what is the richest thing?"

His wife said, "Your bank is the richest thing. There is more money there than anywhere else."

The banker was filled with joy. "You are right, wife!" he said. "You will win a new dress!"

When the tailor got home, he was very sad. His daughter met him at the door.

"What is the matter, Father?" she asked.

The tailor told his daughter about the three questions. "I do not know the answers," he sighed.

The tailor's daughter was a very clever young woman. "Perhaps I can help you," she said.

The next day the tailor got ready to see the judge. As the tailor was leaving, his daughter told him what to say.

When the tailor got to the judge's house, the banker was already there. He looked very happy.

The judge asked the three questions again. "What are your answers?" he asked the banker.

The banker rubbed his hands together.

He felt very important. "Why, my dear man," he said, "the fastest thing in the world? That must be my gray horse, of course. For nothing ever passes us on the road. The sweetest thing? It is the honey that my wife buys in the store. And the richest thing? It is surely my bank. There is more money there than anywhere else."

The banker smiled as though he had already won.

"H'mm," said the young judge. He turned to the tailor. "And what are *your* answers?"

The tailor said, "The fastest thing in the world is a good idea. For nothing travels faster than a good idea. The sweetest thing is sleep. For when you are very tired, there is nothing sweeter than sleep. The richest thing is the earth. For out of the earth come all the riches of the world."

"Good!" cried the judge. "That is very good! The banker must give you five pieces of silver!"

The unhappy banker turned and went home. The judge said to the tailor, "Tell me the truth. Did you think of those answers?"

The tailor could not lie. He said, "I have a very clever young daughter. She told me what to say."

The judge laughed. Then he said, "I would like to meet your daughter. But let me see just how clever she is. Tell her to come to my house. But she must not come at night and not during the day. And she must come to my house without walking or riding."

When the tailor's daughter heard this, she smiled. She said, "Father, go to the market and buy a goat."

The tailor was surprised. But he did what she said.

The tailor's daughter waited until it was dawn. The night was over. But the day had not yet begun. She put one leg over the goat's back. She kept her other leg on the ground. And she went to the judge's house that way.

Did she walk? No. For she went with one leg over the goat. Did she ride? No. For she hopped along on one leg.

Finally, the tailor's daughter reached the judge's house. Then she called out, "Here I am, judge. It is not night. And it is not yet day. And I have come to your house without walking or riding."

The judge was **delighted** with the tailor's daughter. And the tailor's daughter was just as pleased with him. So a short time later the two were married.

The judge said, "Please understand this, my dear wife. I know you are very clever. But when I give people an answer, you must never say I am wrong. If you do, you must go home to your father that day."

All went very well for a time. Then one day
two farmers came to speak to the
judge. One of the farmers owned a
sheep. It gave birth to a lamb. The
lamb ran under the other farmer's
wagon. The farmer who owned the
wagon told the judge, "The lamb
should be mine. After all, it was
under *my* wagon."

The judge was thinking about
something else when he heard the story. He **carelessly**
said, "The farmer who found the lamb under his wagon
should have the lamb."

The farmer who owned the sheep happened to meet the
judge's wife. He stopped to tell her what happened. The
wife knew that her husband was wrong.

She told the farmer, "Come back later this afternoon.
Bring a fishing pole and stand in the middle of the road.
The judge will see you. He will ask what you are doing
there. Say, 'I am catching fish.' He will ask you how you
can catch fish on a dusty road. Say, 'It is as easy for a road
to give fish as it is for a wagon to give birth to a lamb.'
Then he will see he was wrong. He will
give you back your lamb. But do not
let him know that I told you this!"

That afternoon the judge saw a man
fishing in the middle of the road. The
judge said, "Don't you know that you

cannot catch fish in a road?" The man said, "It is as easy for a road to give fish as it is for a wagon to give birth to a lamb."

The judge saw it was the man who owned the sheep. The judge said, "Of course, the lamb belongs to you. I will see that you get it back. But who told you to do this? You did not think of it yourself."

The farmer tried not to tell. But the judge kept questioning him. The judge finally found out that his wife told the farmer what to do.

The judge was very angry. He said to his wife, "Don't you remember what I said? You told the farmer that I was wrong. Now you must go back to your father's house—today! But you may take with you the one thing you like best in my house. For I don't want people to say I was bad to you."

"Very well, my dear husband," said the wife. "I will do as you say. I will go back to my father's house. And I will take with me the one thing I like best in your house. But don't make me go until after supper. We have been very happy together. I would like to eat one more meal with you. Let us be kind to each other—as we have always been. Then let us part as friends."

"That is fine," said the judge.

The wife made a wonderful meal. She made all the foods that her husband liked best. The meal was so good that he ate and ate. And the more he ate, the sleepier he got. Finally, he fell fast asleep in his chair.

The wife carried him out to the wagon that was waiting to take her back to her father.

The next morning the judge opened his eyes. He looked around. He saw that he was in the tailor's house.

"What does this mean?" the judge cried out.

"Nothing, dear husband. It is nothing!" the judge's wife said. "You told me I could take home the one thing I liked best in your house. So, of course, I took you!"

The judge began to laugh. "Dear wife," he said. "Come, let us go home!"

So they got into the wagon and went back to their house.

The judge and his wife lived happily together from that day on.

Now and then someone came to the judge with a very hard problem. Then the judge smiled and said, "We must talk this over with my wife. As you will see, she is very, very clever."

TELL ABOUT THE STORY.

Put an *x* in the box next to the right answer. Each sentence tells a *fact* about the story.

1. The judge asked the two friends to
   - ☐ a. answer three questions.
   - ☐ b. tell him about themselves.
   - ☐ c. explain why each thought he was smarter than the other.

2. The banker's wife thought that the sweetest thing was
   - ☐ a. the cake she made.
   - ☐ b. the honey she bought.
   - ☐ c. sleep, when you are tired.

3. The banker had to give the tailor
   - ☐ a. five pieces of silver.
   - ☐ b. a new dress for his wife.
   - ☐ c. a gray horse.

4. The tailor's daughter said the thing she liked best was
   - ☐ a. the judge's horse.
   - ☐ b. the judge's land.
   - ☐ c. the judge.

ADD WORDS TO SENTENCES.

Complete the sentences below. Fill in each blank with one of the words in the box. Each word can be found in the story. There are five words and four blanks. This means that one word in the box will not be used.

See how clever you are at answering this _____ : What do
₁

_____ find at the end of
₂

everything? Take some _____
₃

to think of the answer. Did you

_____ it right? It is the letter *g*.
₄

> time   question
>   smiled
>   get   you

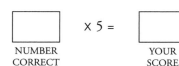

☐ × 5 = ☐	☐ × 5 = ☐
NUMBER CORRECT YOUR SCORE	NUMBER CORRECT YOUR SCORE

LEARN NEW WORDS.

The vocabulary words are printed in **dark type** in the story. You may look back at the words before you answer these questions. Put an *x* in the box next to the right answer.

1. He had to settle the question. As used here, the word *settle* means
   - ☐ a. to live in a place.
   - ☐ b. to try to forget.
   - ☐ c. to give an answer to.

2. He had to decide which man was smarter. When you *decide,* you
   - ☐ a. make up your mind.
   - ☐ b. do not know.
   - ☐ c. get into a fight.

3. They were so delighted with each other that they soon got married. The word *delighted* means
   - ☐ a. very sorry.
   - ☐ b. very worried.
   - ☐ c. very happy.

4. He was thinking about something else and answered carelessly. When you do something *carelessly,* you
   - ☐ a. take a lot of time.
   - ☐ b. are not careful.
   - ☐ c. are always right.

EXPLAIN WHAT HAPPENED.

Here is how to answer these questions. First think about what happened in the story. Then *figure out* (work out) the right answer. This is called *critical thinking.*

1. Which sentence is true?
   - ☐ a. At first, the banker was sure he had won the bet.
   - ☐ b. No one liked the judge.
   - ☐ c. The tailor was rich.

2. The judge's wife probably made all the foods he loved because she
   - ☐ a. knew he was hungry.
   - ☐ b. thought he was too thin.
   - ☐ c. hoped he would eat a lot and then fall asleep.

3. The judge went back home with his wife because he knew she
   - ☐ a. had left some things there.
   - ☐ b. loved him very much.
   - ☐ c. did not like her father.

4. The last lines of the story show that the judge
   - ☐ a. was still angry with his wife.
   - ☐ b. never asked for her help.
   - ☐ c. asked his wife to help him sometimes.

	x 5 =	
NUMBER CORRECT		YOUR SCORE

	x 5 =	
NUMBER CORRECT		YOUR SCORE

SPOT STORY ELEMENTS.

Some story elements are **plot,** **character,** and **setting.** (See page 3.) Put an *x* in the box next to the right answer.

1. What happened first in the *plot*?
   - ☐ a. The judge fell asleep in his chair.
   - ☐ b. The judge gave the lamb to a farmer.
   - ☐ c. Two friends got into a fight about who was smarter.

2. What happened last in the *plot*?
   - ☐ a. The tailor's daughter told her father what to say.
   - ☐ b. The judge woke up in the tailor's house.
   - ☐ c. The judge saw a man fishing in the road.

3. Which sentence best *characterizes* the tailor's daughter?
   - ☐ a. She was a good cook.
   - ☐ b. She helped her father.
   - ☐ c. She was very clever.

4. The story is *set* in
   - ☐ a. a town in Finland.
   - ☐ b. a city in France.
   - ☐ c. a village in Florida.

☐ × 5 = ☐

NUMBER CORRECT   YOUR SCORE

THINK SOME MORE ABOUT THE STORY.

Your teacher might want you to write your answers.

- Explain how the tailor's daughter went to the judge's house without walking or riding.
- Do you think the judge guessed that it was his wife who helped the farmer? Why?
- Make up your own answers to the judge's three questions.

Write your scores in the boxes below. Then write your scores on pages 138 and 139.

☐ **T**ELL ABOUT THE STORY
+
☐ **A**DD WORDS TO SENTENCES
+
☐ **L**EARN NEW WORDS
+
☐ **E**XPLAIN WHAT HAPPENED
+
☐ **S**POT STORY ELEMENTS
=
☐ TOTAL SCORE: Story 8

9
The Man Who Said Moo

a West African folktale

Before You Read

Before you read "The Man Who Said Moo," study the words below. Make sure you know what each word means. This will help you understand the story.

honest: fair; truthful

robbers: people who take things that do not belong to them

describe: to tell how someone or something looks

stole: took something that belongs to someone else

prove: to show that something is true

nodded: moved the head up and down

The Man Who Said Moo

a West African folktale

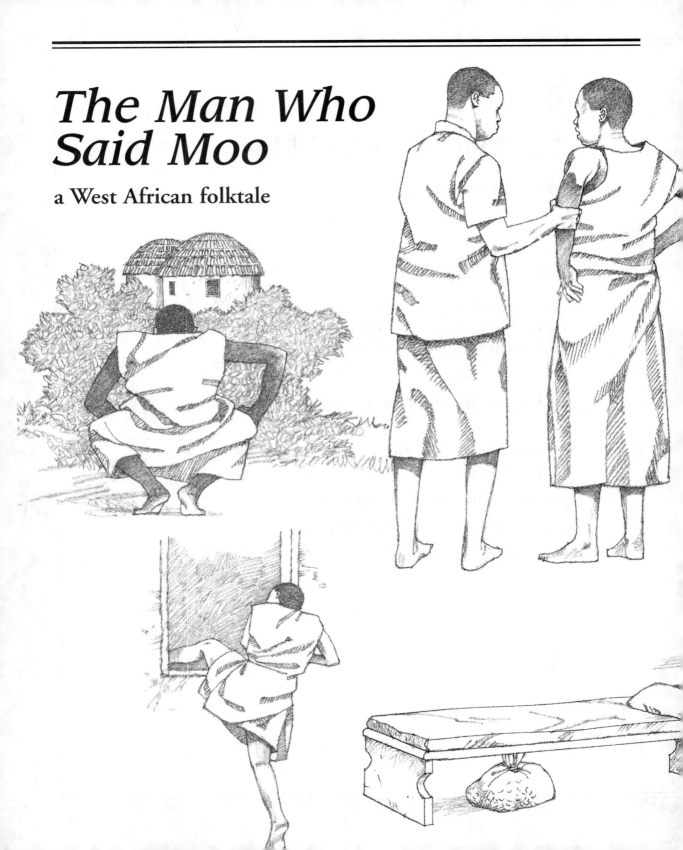

Natafi is a small town in West Africa. The people of Natafi are honest and work very hard. But there were two robbers who lived in the town. Their names were Koto and Adi. They were always trying to find ways to get something for nothing.

A rich man named Biafu moved to Natafi. He lived alone in a house on top of a hill. There was a beautiful garden in front of his house.

One day Koto thought to himself, "Everyone knows that Biafu is very rich. People say that he keeps two bags of gold in his house. I must have some of his gold."

So after dinner, Koto walked up the hill. He went into Biafu's garden and hid behind a bush. Koto waited for a long time. When it was beginning to get dark, Biafu left the house. Koto climbed through a window and **entered** the home.

Koto went from room to room. He looked everywhere. Finally, he found the two bags of gold.

Koto said, "I am very lucky. I will take home the two bags of gold."

Koto tried to lift the bags, but they were too heavy. He could not pick up both bags.

"One bag is better than none," Koto said to himself. "I will take one bag now. I will come back for the other bag some day."

Koto went outside. It was dark, and there was no one around. He took the bag home and put it under his bed. He was very tired, so he went to sleep.

Later that evening, Biafu **returned** to his home. He saw that someone had taken a bag of gold. Biafu looked through the house, but the robber had gone.

The next day Koto took out the bag of gold. He kept looking at the gold. He was very happy and very excited. He said to himself, "I want a fine, new coat. I can buy one now!"

But Koto could not stop thinking about the other bag of gold. He thought, "One bag of gold is good. But two bags are better."

Then Koto told himself, "You must wait a while before you go back to Biafu's house. You must not go back now. That would not be safe. Wait a week or ten days. You can go back then."

But Koto could not wait. He was too **eager** to have that other bag of gold. So that same day he climbed up the hill. He went into the garden and waited behind a bush.

A little later Biafu came out of the house. He began to **wander** through the garden. He was looking at the flowers. Suddenly, he saw Koto behind a bush. Biafu grabbed Koto by the arm.

"What are you doing in my garden?" asked Biafu.

Koto did not know what to say. "I . . . I . . . was taking a walk," Koto finally answered. Biafu looked at Koto. Biafu saw at once that the man was lying. Biafu thought to himself, "This must be the man who stole my gold."

Just then Koto pulled back his arm and ran away.

Biafu went to the judge in the town. Biafu told him the story.

The judge asked Biafu, "What did that man look like?"

Biafu remembered the man very well. He was able to describe him to the judge.

"Ah," said the judge, shaking his head. "I know who you mean. His name is Koto. He has been in trouble before. He may have taken your gold." The judge thought for a moment. Then he said, "I will send for this Koto. I will ask him some questions and see what he says."

The next day a tall policeman came to Koto's place. The policeman told Koto, "Tomorrow at ten o'clock you must see the judge."

Now Koto was very worried. He hurried to his friend, Adi, the other robber.

Koto said, "What should I do? I took a bag of gold from Biafu's house. But later Biafu saw me hiding in his garden. He knows that I must have taken the gold. Tomorrow I must go before the judge. He will ask me many questions. What should I say?"

Adi thought for a while. Then he answered, "I can help you. What will you give me if I do?"

Koto said, "If the judge lets me go, I will give you half the gold."

Adi said, "They cannot prove that you took the gold. But you must not answer any of the judge's questions."

Koto was surprised. "Not answer the judge's questions? How can I do *that?*"

Adi said, "Go home now and put on old rags. Sleep in the rags. Do not wash tomorrow. Do not comb your hair. When the judge asks you questions, smile and say, 'Moo.' Smile at everyone, but always answer, 'Moo.' The judge will think you have gone mad. He will send you home."

Koto did that. To every question the judge asked, Koto said, "Moo." Koto smiled at the judge. He smiled at the tall policeman who sat next to the judge. But he always answered, "Moo."

The judge got angry. Finally, he told Koto to go.

As the happy Koto was leaving, the judge turned to the tall policeman and whispered something in his ear.

Later that day, Adi came to Koto's place. Adi said, "I see that the judge let you go."

Koto smiled and said, "Moo."

Adi said, "Now give me my gold."

Koto smiled and said, "Moo."

To everything Adi said, Koto answered, "Moo." Finally, Adi went home without any gold.

The happy Koto said, "Now I will buy a new coat!" He went to a store.

"May I help you?" asked the owner.

Koto was just about to answer. But then he saw the tall policeman, who had followed him into the store.

Koto thought to himself, "They are trying to trick me. I better keep saying, 'Moo.'"

"May I help you?" said the owner again.

Koto smiled, shook his head, and said, "Moo."

"What would you like to see?" asked the man.

Koto pointed to a coat and said, "Moo."

"Would you like to try that on?"

Koto nodded yes and said, "Moo."

Koto put on the coat. He had never seen such a beautiful coat! And it fit so well! He could not take his eyes off the coat.

Koto looked at himself in the mirror. He had never looked so good.

"My!" said Koto to the owner. "Don't I look fine?"

"Very fine!" said the tall policeman. And an hour later, Koto was standing in front of the judge.

TELL ABOUT THE STORY.

Put an *x* in the box next to the right answer. Each sentence tells a *fact* about the story.

1. Koto went to Biafu's house to
   - ☐ a. have dinner.
   - ☐ b. see the flowers in his garden.
   - ☐ c. take his gold.

2. The judge said that Koto
   - ☐ a. had never been in any trouble.
   - ☐ b. had been in trouble before.
   - ☐ c. was liked by everyone.

3. Adi told Koto to
   - ☐ a. stay away from the judge.
   - ☐ b. smile and say, "Moo."
   - ☐ c. leave town at once.

4. Koto went to a store to buy
   - ☐ a. a coat.
   - ☐ b. some food.
   - ☐ c. a hat.

ADD WORDS TO SENTENCES.

Complete the sentences below. Fill in each blank with one of the words in the box. Each word can be found in the story. There are five words and four blanks. This means that one word in the box will not be used.

A long time ago, _____ believed there was a place called El Dorado. It was supposed to be a land that was covered with _____. Over the years, _____ people have found gold here and there. But no one has ever _____ El Dorado.

found	gold
lucky	
followed	people

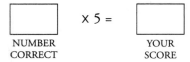

NUMBER CORRECT   X 5 =   YOUR SCORE

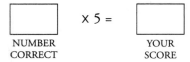

NUMBER CORRECT   X 5 =   YOUR SCORE

119

LEARN NEW WORDS.

The vocabulary words are printed in **dark type** in the story. You may look back at the words before you answer these questions. Put an *x* in the box next to the right answer.

1. He climbed through a window and entered the house. The word *entered* means
   - ☐ a. found.
   - ☐ b. showed.
   - ☐ c. went into.

2. Biafu returned to his home that evening. The word *returned* means
   - ☐ a. saw at once.
   - ☐ b. came back.
   - ☐ c. fixed.

3. Koto was eager to get the gold. When you are *eager,* you
   - ☐ a. are not in a hurry.
   - ☐ b. want something very much.
   - ☐ c. feel very sad.

4. Biafu began to wander through his garden. The word *wander* means
   - ☐ a. move slowly about.
   - ☐ b. run very quickly.
   - ☐ c. fall to the ground.

EXPLAIN WHAT HAPPENED.

Here is how to answer these questions. First think about what happened in the story. Then *figure out* (work out) the right answer. This is called *critical thinking.*

1. Which sentence is true?
   - ☐ a. Biafu was not rich.
   - ☐ b. Koto could not wait to get the other bag of gold.
   - ☐ c. Koto gave Adi some gold.

2. Adi's plan was to
   - ☐ a. prove that Koto did not take the gold.
   - ☐ b. show that Koto was smart.
   - ☐ c. keep Koto from answering the judge's questions.

3. Koto began to speak at the store because he
   - ☐ a. did not see the policeman.
   - ☐ b. wanted to pay for the coat.
   - ☐ c. thought he looked good.

4. The last lines of the story seem to say that Koto will
   - ☐ a. not get away this time.
   - ☐ b. trick the judge.
   - ☐ c. keep saying, "Moo."

☐ × 5 = ☐

NUMBER CORRECT   YOUR SCORE

☐ × 5 = ☐

NUMBER CORRECT   YOUR SCORE

SPOT STORY ELEMENTS.

Some story elements are **plot, character,** and **setting.** (See page 3.) Put an *x* in the box next to the right answer.

1. What happened first in the *plot*?
   - ☐ a. Koto put on a beautiful coat.
   - ☐ b. The judge told Koto to go.
   - ☐ c. Biafu moved to Natafi.

2. What happened last in the *plot*?
   - ☐ a. Koto said, "Don't I look fine?"
   - ☐ b. Adi told Koto to dress in rags.
   - ☐ c. Koto found two bags of gold.

3. Who is the *main character* in the story?
   - ☐ a. Adi
   - ☐ b. Koto
   - ☐ c. the tall policeman

4. Where is the story *set*?
   - ☐ a. in a large, busy city
   - ☐ b. in a town in West Africa
   - ☐ c. in a village in the United States

☐ × 5 = ☐

NUMBER CORRECT   YOUR SCORE

THINK SOME MORE ABOUT THE STORY.

Your teacher might want you to write your answers.

- Why did Biafu think that the man in the garden had taken the gold? Give as many reasons as you can.
- What do you think the judge whispered in the tall policeman's ear?
- Do you think the story had a good ending? Explain your answer.

Write your scores in the boxes below. Then write your scores on pages 138 and 139.

☐ **T**ELL ABOUT THE STORY
+
☐ **A**DD WORDS TO SENTENCES
+
☐ **L**EARN NEW WORDS
+
☐ **E**XPLAIN WHAT HAPPENED
+
☐ **S**POT STORY ELEMENTS
=
☐ TOTAL SCORE: Story 9

10

Hercules and the Three Golden Apples

by Nathaniel Hawthorne, from a Greek myth

Before You Read

Before you read "Hercules and the Three Golden Apples," study the words below. Make sure you know what each word means. This will help you understand the story.

myth: an old story; a story from the past

hero: a brave person who does great things for others

crush: break into pieces

huge: very big

floated: As used in this story, the word means "moved slowly through the air."

Hercules and the Three Golden Apples

by Nathaniel Hawthorne, from a Greek myth

There is a Greek myth about a wonderful garden. Apples made of gold grew on a tree in the garden. Children loved to listen to this story. They thought that when they grew up, they would find the garden. They would go there and bring back some golden apples.

Brave young men looked for the garden. Many of them never came back. Those who returned never brought back any golden apples. No wonder they were not able to **gather** the apples! It is said that a terrible dragon sat under

125

the tree. It had one hundred heads. Fifty heads were always awake. They watched the tree, while the other fifty heads slept.

Once, a great hero traveled through the land. He was taller and stronger than any man. He was dressed in the skin of the biggest lion that ever lived. He carried a club in his hand. And across his back was a bow with a holder for arrows.

As he went on his way, he met many people. He would say, "I am looking for the Garden of the Golden Apples. Is this the right road to that garden?"

No one was able to answer his question. Some might have laughed at the man. But he was tall and strong. And he carried a big club!

So he traveled on and on. At last, he came to a lovely green field. He saw some beautiful young women. They were picking flowers.

He asked, "Is this the way to the Garden of the Golden Apples?"

The young women were surprised.

"The Garden of the Golden Apples!" cried one. "No one has ever come back from that garden! Please tell us, dear traveler, what do you want from that garden?"

The traveler answered, "The king has ordered me to bring him three golden apples. I must listen to the king."

Another woman said, "Do you know that a dragon with a hundred heads waits under that tree?"

"I know that well," the traveler said. "But ever since I was a boy, it has been my business to face **danger**."

"Go back!" they all cried. "Go back to your home! Your mother will cry tears of joy when she sees you again. Forget about the golden apples! Do not listen to the king! We do not wish the dragon with a hundred heads to kill you!"

The traveler lifted his club. He let it fall against a rock. The rock flew into a hundred pieces.

The young man smiled. He said, "Do you not think a blow like that would crush one of the dragon's hundred heads?"

Then he sat on the grass. He told them the story of his life. When he was still a baby, two giant snakes crawled toward him on the floor. He grabbed the snakes and squeezed both of them to death.

When he was just a boy, he killed a mountain lion. Later, he had to fight an ugly monster. It was called a hydra. The hydra had nine heads. There were long, sharp teeth in every one of them.

One woman said, "But the dragon in the garden has *one hundred* heads!"

The young man said, "I would rather fight *two* dragons than one hydra. For as soon as I cut off a hydra's head, two other heads grew back in its place."

The young man went on, "It was not possible to kill the hydra. So I buried it deep in the earth. I put a heavy stone above the spot. The hydra cannot get away. It cannot cause any more trouble now."

The young man told them many other stories. He once chased a deer for twelve months. He never stopped to catch his breath. At last, he caught it by the horns. Then he brought it home.

Another time he **tamed** a thousand horses that were running wild. Once, he caught a bull and let it go. Another time he turned around a river.

Finally, he finished telling his adventures. "You may have heard of me," he said. "My name is Hercules!"

"We had already guessed that," said the women. "Your **deeds** are known around the world. We no longer think it strange that you are looking for the Garden of the Golden Apples."

They gave him bread and grapes to eat. Then one of the women said, "We will tell you how to find the Garden of the Golden Apples. Go down to the sea. You will find the Old One there. You will know him by his long green beard. Ask him where the Golden Garden is."

"The Old One?" said Hercules.

"He is the Old Man of the Sea. He knows where the Golden Garden is. It is on an island far away."

Hercules thanked them for the bread and grapes. He thanked them for telling him about the Old One.

As he left, one of the women called to him, "Hercules! Remember this! Grab the Old One when you see him! Hold him tightly! Do not let him go!"

"I will remember that," said Hercules. Then he went to find the Old One.

Hercules came to a forest. It was filled with tall, thick trees. Hercules was in a hurry. He swung his club. Down fell the trees. He kept marching on.

Suddenly, he heard a sound. It was the rushing of the sea. Then he saw the water. He saw an old man sleeping on the sand. The old man had a long green beard.

Hercules was glad to find the man asleep. He grabbed him by an arm and a leg. He held the Old One very tightly.

"Tell me!" cried Hercules. "How can I find the Garden of the Golden Apples?"

The Old One woke up right away. He was surprised.

A moment later, Hercules was the one to be surprised. He held the Old One very tightly. But suddenly the Old One changed! He turned into a large wild bull. It roared. It kicked at Hercules! But Hercules held on to it! He would not let the wild bull go.

Then the wild bull changed into an ugly dog with three huge heads. Each head was filled with long, sharp teeth. It barked and snapped at Hercules. It bit his hands. But Hercules still held on to it.

Suddenly, the dog disappeared. In its place there was a snake. Hercules had once killed a giant snake. But this snake was fifty times as big! It wrapped itself around Hercules. It squeezed as hard as it could squeeze. But Hercules held on.

The Old One could change himself into anything. But no matter what he did, Hercules held on. He would not let go!

Finally, the Old One cried, "Who are you? What do you want with me?"

"My name is Hercules!" he roared.

"I thought as much," the Old One said.

"And I will never let you go," said Hercules, "until you tell me how to find the Garden of the Golden Apples."

The Old One knew he could not get away. He told Hercules what path to take. The Old One said, "Go along the path until you find a giant by the sea. He is the greatest giant that you ever saw. He is so tall that he holds the sky upon his head. He knows where the Golden Garden is. He can tell you—if he *wishes* to tell you."

Hercules shook his club. He said, "I will make him tell me. Good-bye. I am sorry that I held you so tightly."

Hercules traveled on the path all night. The next day he came upon the giant. Hercules had never seen so great a giant! He was as big as any mountain. He was so tall that clouds floated past his face. And on his head he held the sky!

Poor man! He must have been standing there for many years. A forest grew around his legs. Trees had pushed up between his toes.

The giant looked at Hercules. "Who are you down there!" he roared.

"I am Hercules!" a voice roared back. "I am looking for the Garden of the Golden Apples."

"HO!" roared the giant. Then he began to laugh.

"Why do you laugh?" cried Hercules. "Do you think I fear the dragon with a hundred heads?"

The giant did not answer. He only shouted, "I am Atlas—the greatest giant in the world! I hold the sky upon my head!"

"So I see," said Hercules. "But can you tell me how to find the Golden Garden?"

"What do you want there?" Atlas asked.

"Three golden apples. I must have them for the king."

The giant shouted, "Only *I* can get apples from the Golden Garden!"

Atlas looked down at Hercules and said, "The garden is on an island in the sea behind me. I would be glad to get the apples for you. But I must stand here holding up the sky."

"I see," said Hercules. "Why don't you put the sky down on a mountain?"

"I would like to," Atlas said. "But there is no mountain high enough. You know, if you stood on top of that mountain there, you would be just as tall as I am. You seem very strong. Why don't *you* hold up the sky for a while? Then I can get the golden apples for you."

Hercules *was* very strong. But was he strong enough to hold up the sky? For once, Hercules was a little worried.

"How heavy is the sky?" he asked.

"It is very heavy," Atlas said.

Hercules then asked, "How long will it take you to get the golden apples?"

"Oh, just a few minutes," Atlas answered. "I can go ten miles with each step I take."

"Well, then," said Hercules, "I will climb that tall mountain there!"

Hercules was very kind. He wanted to let Atlas rest for a little while. And Hercules *liked* the idea of holding up the sky! That was much harder than killing a dragon with a hundred heads! So Atlas lifted up the sky. Then he put it down on Hercules's head.

Atlas was very happy. First he lifted one foot out of the forest. Then he lifted his other foot. Then he jumped into the air with joy. He came down with a bang that made the world shake.

Atlas stepped out into the sea behind him. It was true. He could cover ten miles with each step. In just a few minutes, the giant was gone.

Hercules began to worry. He thought to himself, "What will I do if Atlas is killed by the dragon? How will I ever get rid of the sky on my head? I will have to hold up the sky forever!"

But soon Hercules saw the giant. He was coming closer! And he was holding three golden apples!

"I am glad to see you again," said Hercules. "I see you have brought back three golden apples."

"Of course!" answered Atlas. "I took the best that grew on the tree. The garden is a very beautiful place. And the dragon with a hundred heads is well worth seeing. You would have liked getting the apples yourself."

"It does not matter," said Hercules. "You did the job well. Now I have a long way to go. I am in a hurry. The king is waiting for the golden apples. Please take the sky and put it back on your head."

"What is the rush?" asked Atlas. "I held up the sky for more than a thousand years. I will let you hold it up for a thousand years too. Then maybe I will take it back."

"What!" said Hercules. He angrily shook his head. When he did, two or three stars fell out of their place in the sky.

"Oh, that will never do!" Atlas laughed. "You must be careful with those stars!"

"Well then," said Hercules. "Take back the sky for two minutes, please. I want to take off the bow and arrows around my back. If I must stand here for a thousand years, I must make myself more comfortable."

"That is fair enough," Atlas said. "I will take back the sky for two minutes then. But just for two minutes. Remember that!"

Atlas threw the apples down on the ground. He lifted the sky from Hercules's head. Then he put the sky back on his own head.

Hercules picked up the three golden apples and started for home.

"Come back! Come back!" the giant yelled. But Hercules did not stop. He went on his way.

The giant stands there to this day.

Now and then, you may hear the sound of thunder. That is Atlas's angry voice. He is still shouting for Hercules to come back.

TELL ABOUT THE STORY.

Put an *x* in the box next to the right answer. Each sentence tells a *fact* about the story.

1. The dragon in the Golden Garden had
   - ☐ a. only one head.
   - ☐ b. about fifty heads.
   - ☐ c. one hundred heads.

2. The Old One was able to
   - ☐ a. change himself into anything.
   - ☐ b. make Hercules let go of him.
   - ☐ c. make Hercules go back home.

3. Atlas's job was to
   - ☐ a. fight dragons.
   - ☐ b. kill snakes.
   - ☐ c. hold up the sky.

4. Atlas came back from the garden with
   - ☐ a. beautiful flowers.
   - ☐ b. three golden apples.
   - ☐ c. the dragon.

ADD WORDS TO SENTENCES.

Complete the sentences below. Fill in each blank with one of the words in the box. Each word can be found in the story. There are five words and four blanks. This means that one word in the box will not be used.

One Greek myth tells the story of a man named _____. In the
1
_____, Hercules is given twelve
2
jobs, or tasks, to do. Each one is very hard or is filled with _____.
3
But the _____ Hercules is able
4
to do each task.

myth   Hercules
caught
danger   great

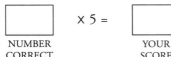

NUMBER CORRECT   x 5 =   YOUR SCORE

NUMBER CORRECT   x 5 =   YOUR SCORE

135

LEARN NEW WORDS.

The vocabulary words are printed in **dark type** in the story. You may look back at the words before you answer these questions. Put an *x* in the box next to the right answer.

1. He, alone, could gather apples from the Golden Garden. The word *gather* means
   - ☐ a. try to buy.
   - ☐ b. pick and bring together.
   - ☐ c. lose everything.

2. Hercules said, "It has been my business to face danger." When you face *danger,* you
   - ☐ a. can get hurt.
   - ☐ b. do not speak.
   - ☐ c. play games.

3. Hercules tamed horses. Animals that have been *tamed* are
   - ☐ a. no longer wild.
   - ☐ b. wilder than ever.
   - ☐ c. very hungry.

4. His deeds were well known around the world. What are *deeds?*
   - ☐ a. friends
   - ☐ b. good wishes
   - ☐ c. things that someone does

EXPLAIN WHAT HAPPENED.

Here is how to answer these questions. First think about what happened in the story. Then *figure out* (work out) the right answer. This is called *critical thinking.*

1. The women guessed that the man was Hercules because
   - ☐ a. they had seen him before.
   - ☐ b. they knew he was coming.
   - ☐ c. only Hercules could have done all those great things.

2. The women did not
   - ☐ a. give Hercules bread.
   - ☐ b. give Hercules apples.
   - ☐ c. tell Hercules where to find the Old One.

3. Which sentence is true?
   - ☐ a. Hercules was taller than Atlas.
   - ☐ b. Hercules was willing to give Atlas some rest.
   - ☐ c. Hercules dropped the sky.

4. It is fair to say that Hercules
   - ☐ a. tricked Atlas.
   - ☐ b. was afraid of Atlas.
   - ☐ c. was willing to hold up the sky forever.

	× 5 =	
NUMBER CORRECT		YOUR SCORE

	× 5 =	
NUMBER CORRECT		YOUR SCORE

SPOT STORY ELEMENTS.

Some story elements are **plot**, **character,** and **setting.** (See page 3.) Put an *x* in the box next to the right answer.

1. What happened last in the *plot*?
   - ☐ a. Hercules killed a very large snake.
   - ☐ b. Hercules saw the Old One sleeping.
   - ☐ c. Hercules picked up the golden apples.

2. Who is the *main character* in the story?
   - ☐ a. Atlas
   - ☐ b. the Old One
   - ☐ c. Hercules

3. Which sentence best *characterizes* Hercules?
   - ☐ a. He was never kind.
   - ☐ b. He was very brave.
   - ☐ c. He was not brave.

4. The story is *set*
   - ☐ a. a long time ago.
   - ☐ b. a few years ago.
   - ☐ c. today.

	× 5 =	
NUMBER CORRECT		YOUR SCORE

THINK SOME MORE ABOUT THE STORY.

Your teacher might want you to write your answers.

- What were some of the wonderful things that Hercules did? Think of as many as you can.
- Do you think Hercules would have been able to get the apples from the Golden Garden? Why?
- Suppose the dragon had killed Hercules. How do you think the story would have ended?

Write your scores in the boxes below. Then write your scores on pages 138 and 139.

☐	**T**ELL ABOUT THE STORY
+	
☐	**A**DD WORDS TO SENTENCES
+	
☐	**L**EARN NEW WORDS
+	
☐	**E**XPLAIN WHAT HAPPENED
+	
☐	**S**POT STORY ELEMENTS
=	
☐	TOTAL SCORE: Story 10

Progress Chart

1. Write in your score for each exercise.
2. Write in your TOTAL SCORE.

	T	A	L	E	S	TOTAL SCORE
Story 1						
Story 2						
Story 3						
Story 4						
Story 5						
Story 6						
Story 7						
Story 8						
Story 9						
Story 10						

Progress Graph

1. Write your TOTAL SCORE in the box under the number for each story.
2. Put an *x* along the line above each box to show your TOTAL SCORE for that story.
3. Make a graph of your progress by drawing a line to connect the *x*'s.

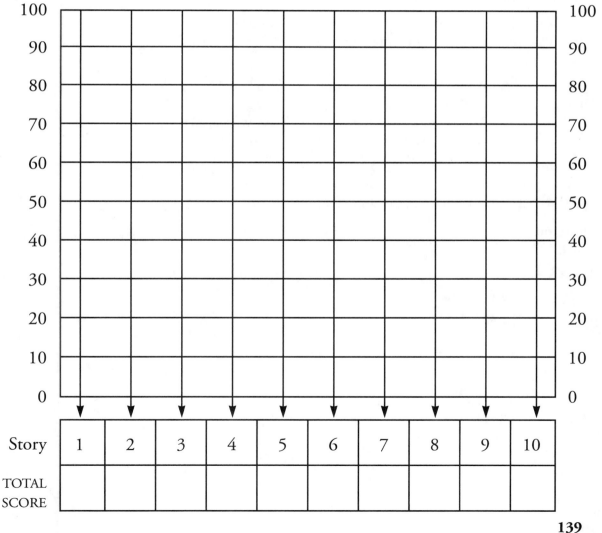

Acknowledgments

Text:
Acknowledgment is gratefully made to the following publishers, authors, and agents for permission to reprint these works. Every effort has been made to determine copyright owners. In the case of any omissions, the Publisher will be pleased to make suitable acknowledgments in future editions.

"Good Advice" from *The Day It Snowed Tortillas: Tales from Spanish New Mexico* retold by Joe Hayes. Reprinted by permission of Mariposa Printing & Publishing, Santa Fe, New Mexico.

"The Wild Winds of Wok" from *The Whirly Winds of Wok* by Dorothy Tofte. Reprinted by permission of Larry Sternig/Jack Byrne Literary Agency.

"The Tale of the Wolf" from "The Wolf of Chungshan" by Lin Yutang from *Famous Chinese Short Stories* by Lin Yutang. Copyright © 1948, 1951, 1952 by (John Day Co.) Harper & Row Publishers, Inc. Reprinted by permission of Taiyi Lin Lai and Hsiang Ju Lin.

"The Man Who Said Moo" based on the story "The Robbers and the Old Man." Collected in *West African Folk-tales* by W. H. Barker and C. Sinclair. George G. Harrap and Company, London, 1917.

Illustrations:
David Cunningham
Yoshi Miyake